Understanding Man's Best Friend

WHY DOGS LOOK AND ACT THE WAY THEY DO

by Dr. Ann Squire

Macmillan Publishing Company   New York
Collier Macmillan Canada   Toronto
Maxwell Macmillan International Publishing Group
New York   Oxford   Singapore   Sydney

By the same author

101 Questions and Answers About Pets and People

Copyright © 1991 by Ann Squire
All rights reserved. No part of this book may be reproduced or transmitted in any form or by any means, electronic or mechanical, including photocopying, recording, or by any information storage and retrieval system, without permission in writing from the Publisher.
Macmillan Publishing Company
866 Third Avenue
New York, NY 10022
Collier Macmillan Canada, Inc.
1200 Eglinton Avenue East
Suite 200
Don Mills, Ontario M3C 3N1
First edition
Printed in the United States of America
10 9 8 7 6 5 4 3 2 1

The text of this book is set in 12 point Sabon.
Book design by Constance Ftera.

Library of Congress Cataloging-in-Publication Data
Squire, Ann.
Understanding man's best friend: why dogs look and act the way they do / by Ann Squire.—1st American ed.
    p.   cm.
Summary: Looks at the similarities and differences among different breeds of dogs.
ISBN 0-02-786590-8
1. Dogs—History—Juvenile literature. 2. Dog breeds—Juvenile literature. 3. Dogs—Behavior—Juvenile literature. [1. Dogs— History. 2. Dog breeds. 3. Dogs—Habits and behavior.]
I. Title.
SF426.5.S68   1991   636.7—dc20   90-30631   CIP   AC

To Jeff,
who encouraged me to write this book

and to Bunny,
who accepted the project
with feline good grace.

Contents

Introduction ... vii

PART ONE   Becoming Best Friends:
           The History of Dogs and People ... 1

  1 In the Beginning ... 3
  2 From Wolf to Dog ... 8
  3 The Dog Becomes a Specialist ... 11
  4 Guards, Hunters, and Pets ... 16

PART TWO   Wolves and Dogs ... 27

  5 A Wolf Tale ... 29
  6 Wolf in Dog's Clothing:
     Understanding Your Pet's Behavior ... 42

PART THREE   Why Is a Dachshund Different
             from a Doberman? ... 49

  7 Picking the Right Dog ... 51
  8 Hard Labor: The Working Breeds ... 53

9	Bringing in the Sheep: The Herding Breeds	65
10	To the Hunt: The Hounds	73
11	Bird Dogs *Extraordinaire*: The Sporting Breeds	81
12	Feisty Fighters: The Terriers	90
13	Just Friends: The Companion Breeds	97

PART FOUR   Pit Bulls and Pekingese: What We've Done to Dogs   103

14	Dog Problems	105

Appendix   Dog Breeds and Their Original Uses   112

Index   117

Introduction

The history of dogs is a fascinating one. Of all domestic species, the dog is our closest companion and is certainly the species that has been with people the longest. Because of human intervention, there are more variations on the dog theme than there are for any other animal. Within just one species, there are over one hundred distinct breeds, differing widely in size, shape, personality, and behavior. Underneath all these differences, though, are certain characteristics that all dogs share. This book will take a look at the similarities—and the differences—among different breeds of dog and will talk about what they mean for you and your pet.

PART ONE

Becoming Best Friends: The History of Dogs and People

1

In the Beginning

Man's best friend. What animal comes to mind when you hear that phrase? A duck? A cow? A garter snake? Of course not. Everyone knows that the nickname "man's best friend" rightfully belongs to the domestic dog. What some people don't know is that, in addition to being man's best friend, the dog is also man's oldest friend. Dogs and people have been partners for thousands of years. In fact, scientists believe that the dog was the very first animal to be domesticated by early humans. The long process of domestication probably took place during the Mesolithic era, which began in around 12,000 B.C.

Compared to the dog, other domestic animals are relative newcomers to life with humans. The cat, for example, was domesticated by the Egyptians in about 3500 B.C. By then, dogs had been living and working with people for several thousand years!

THE HUMAN–DOG PARTNERSHIP: HOW IT MAY HAVE STARTED

What was it about the dog (or, more accurately, the wolf, ancestor of all modern-day dogs) that made it such a good candidate for life with humans?

The truth is that no one really knows. In fact, scientists can't even say for certain what the world was like thousands of years ago. But by studying fossil remains excavated from archaeological sites, they can make some pretty good guesses.

Of all the reasons humans had for choosing the wolf as a companion, the simplest may have been that the wolf was in the right place at the right time. During the Ice Age, which lasted from about 60,000 B.C. to 12,000 B.C., humans are thought to have been nomadic hunters, wandering the tundra in search of big game and never settling in one place for too long. But this vagabond life-style did not last forever. By around 12,000 B.C. (the beginning of the Mesolithic era), the earth was getting warmer and the Ice Age was drawing to a close. The land began to change and people were forced to change with it. No longer could they travel the tundra in search of game, for much of the open land was being overgrown with thick, dense forests. The large animals that had once roamed the plains were disappearing, replaced by secretive forest animals that knew how to hide. With each passing year it grew more difficult for people to live as hunters. If they were to survive, they would have to find other ways of getting food.

So Mesolithic hunters began to change their way of life. They learned to catch fish, to collect oysters and mussels from the sea, and to gather edible plants. At the same time they practiced hunting the elusive animals of the forest.

One effect of this change in life-style was that people no longer had to travel far and wide in search of food. On the contrary, once they found a good fishing spot or a grove of tasty plants, they were much better off staying in one place. So Mesolithic people began to give up their wandering ways and settle down in permanent communities. The settlements formed by these early humans were very primitive. But, small as they were, they had some of the same problems as modern cities. One of these problems was: what to do with the garbage?

And this is where the wolf came in. Like humans, wolves are basically hunters. But, again like humans, wolves don't want to work any harder than they have to. If a wolf pack could survive by hanging around human communities and feeding off leftovers, that was certainly easier than chasing after prey. So some wolves became scavengers, filling their stomachs and, at the same time, keeping the settlements free of garbage. In return for this service, wolves were tolerated, rather than hunted, by humans.

Little by little, people probably got used to the wolves that spent time near their camps. Perhaps they even began to enjoy the animals' company and occasionally tossed them scraps of food. When wolf puppies were born in the spring, humans may have raided the dens and picked out several of the pups to raise as pets. It was probably then that people realized just how much they had in common with these wild canids. ("Canid" refers to animals in the family Canidae, to which both wolves and dogs belong.)

Like people, wolves are very sociable. Both wolves and people live in groups, cooperate with each other in getting food and raising young, and have various ways of communicating among themselves. Wolves, dogs, and humans even communicate in some of the same ways. Sounds (barking and howling for dogs and wolves; talking for people) and body language are two of these shared communication systems.

Both wolves and people have organized societies, where one or two individuals are the leaders and the rest are followers. In a wolf pack, there are often two leaders, one male and one female. They are called the "alpha" wolves and they have time-tested ways of keeping the other pack members in line. In a human family, the parents are usually alpha. Like wolves, they have many ways of reminding their children who's in charge.

Wolves and humans are also alike in their ability to adapt to new situations. People survived after the Ice Age because they found new ways of getting food when hunting became too difficult. If they had not been able to do this, the human species might have died out.

Wolves, too, changed their behavior when a new food source appeared by becoming scavengers at human settlements. Because they were so adaptable, wolves had little trouble adjusting to life with people.

But the thing that was probably the most important for domestication was the fact that wolves, like humans, form strong bonds with their pack (or family) when they are babies. So when Mesolithic tribes adopted and raised wolf puppies, the young animals became attached to people and learned to think of the human group as their pack. The next step was to convince the wolf pup to accept a person as the alpha member of the pack. If this could be accomplished, the hand-raised wolves became much easier to live with when they grew up. Needless to say, the only wolves that stayed on as pets were those who could be taught that man was boss. (What worked with wolves in Mesolithic times still works with dogs. To this day, creating a "leader-follower" relationship between owner and pet is one of the secrets of successful dog training.)

Once people began to raise wolf pups, they discovered some unexpected benefits. Not only did these wolves think of people as their pack, they thought of the settlement as their territory. As we'll see later, wolves are very protective of the area around their dens, and are quick to drive away intruders. When this territory-guarding behavior was transferred to the human settlement, wolves became the world's first watchdogs!

Before too long, people realized that wolves could help them out with yet another job: hunting. We saw that hunters found it almost impossible to track animals in dense forests. Wolves, however, with their keen sense of smell, good hearing, and superior running ability, could find and capture forest animals without much difficulty. They were also good at "sizing up" a herd of reindeer or wild sheep, spotting the weak or old animals, and chasing them until the victims became separated from the herd. These hunting skills, more than anything else, made the wolf an indispensable member of the human group.

2

From Wolf to Dog

Up until now we've been talking only about wolves. When did tamed wolves become domestic dogs? And how did it happen?

Humans began to domesticate wolves during the Mesolithic era. But there is a big difference between even the tamest wolf and a domestic dog. Wolves didn't turn into dogs overnight. It was a gradual metamorphosis, which took place over many generations.

The way people transformed their tame wolves into domestic dogs was through a process called selective breeding. When people found a wolf that looked or acted in a way they liked, they kept that animal and mated it with another wolf that looked or acted the same way. Wolves that didn't fit the bill were not bred.

Suppose, for example, that people decided they liked long-haired wolves better than short-haired wolves. By using selective breeding, they could "create" a new race of wolves with long hair. Here's how it works: In an average group of wolves, some animals have slightly longer hair than others. From this group a wolf breeder would choose the male and female with the longest hair and mate those two animals together. The wolf pups with the longest hair would be mated together or mated with other long-haired wolves. None of the short-haired wolves would be allowed to mate at all. As short-haired wolves died out without having pups, long-haired wolves would become more and more common. Eventually, all the wolves in the group would have long hair. It was through this process of selective breeding (*selecting* a particular look or behavior and *breeding* only the animals that show that characteristic) that wolves gradually turned into domestic dogs.

The first thing people looked for when they began to domesticate the wolf was an animal that was willing to accept a person as "top dog" (or "alpha wolf"). A wolf that refused to share its catch with humans, for instance, wouldn't be much help as a hunter. So people bred only those wolves that they could control. For the same reason, they selected wolves that were small and that had less threatening teeth. After several generations, tame wolves began to look distinctly different from their wild cousins. They were smaller, had less powerful jaws and smaller teeth, and were friendlier and less aggressive around people.

There were other differences as well. A notable one was the shape of the tail. Wild wolves have straight tails that they hold down toward the ground. At some point a tame wolf must have been born with a curly tail, and humans selectively bred these curly tailed animals. Why? Perhaps the tail shape gave people an easy way of telling wild wolves from tame ones. Perhaps a curly tail was easier to spot as the wolf hunted in the tall grass. Or maybe people just liked the way it looked. Whatever the original reason, the curly tail became a universal feature of domestic dogs. To this day, all dogs have curly tails (if they have tails) and all wild canids, such as wolves, foxes, and coyotes, have straight ones.

Two other features that appeared in tame wolves were selected by humans. One was a drooping ear. While all wild canids have pointed ears that stick straight up, many dogs have ears that hang limply at the sides of the head. The fact that all dogs don't have drooping ears tells us that this characteristic appeared later in the domestication process. Some dogs, such as huskies and German shepherds, have kept the wolf's pointed ears while others, such as cocker spaniels and basset hounds, have the "newer," floppy type of ear.

A final, and very important, characteristic of domestic dogs is that they bark a lot. Wolves almost never bark, except when they are puppies. It's certainly better to have a watchdog (or "watchwolf") that barks than one that's silent. So humans probably bred only those wolves that continued to bark when they were adults. Like the curly tail, barking is an almost universal dog characteristic. Except for the basenji, all modern-day dogs bark.

After many generations of selective breeding by humans, the differences between tame and wild wolves began to outweigh the similarities. With their small stature, curly tails, and small teeth, these new animals looked quite different from their wild relatives. What's more, they acted differently from wolves. They were friendly and cooperative with humans, they guarded their villages, and, to top it off, they barked! People didn't really think of them as wolves anymore. They thought of them as something different . . . as dogs. And this is how a new species, *Canis familiaris* (the domestic dog), came into being more than twelve thousand years ago.

3

The Dog Becomes a Specialist

Was that the end of the dog's story? Far from it. Domestication was only the first chapter in the history of dogs and humans. Once people learned how to change dogs through selective breeding, they were able to create "customized" dogs to suit their every need.

And what a lot of needs they had! The more time people spent around dogs, the more jobs they found for them to do. Human society was developing rapidly and this created new occupations for people, as well as for their dogs.

Dogs continued to act as scavengers, living off the leftovers of a growing human civilization. Semi-wild dogs known as pariah dogs still perform this job in some cities in India and the Middle East.

In the icy polar regions, dogs were put to work as draft animals, hauling sledloads of people and their possessions over the frozen ground. To this day, Siberian huskies are used as sled dogs, though working dog teams are quickly being replaced by snowmobiles. With their pointed ears and muzzles and their thick fur, the polar dogs—huskies, Alaskan malamutes, and Samoyeds—look very

Even in ancient times, dogs had been partners with people for thousands of years.

much like their wolf ancestors. In fact, northern tribes sometimes even crossbred their husky sled dogs with wild wolves. The resulting wolf-dogs were thought to be especially strong and resistant to the cold.

Hunting was another important job. But while wolves and early dogs had used all their senses—sight, hearing, and smell—to hunt, humans now began to breed dogs that specialized in different types of hunting. Dogs that were used to track prey through dense forests needed to have a superior sense of smell. Therefore they

In this detail from a sixteenth-century tapestry, dogs help track game through a dense forest.

were chosen and bred for their ability to follow a scent trail. The bloodhound, with its legendary tracking skill, is one descendant of these early scent hounds.

In the flat, open country of the Middle East, gazelles and other fleet-footed animals were the main targets of human hunters. These hunters needed dogs that could spot a gazelle from far away and then run fast enough to catch it. For such dogs, keen vision and a lightweight body built for speed were all-important; a good sense of smell was less useful. Because of their excellent vision, these dogs came to be called sight hounds, or gaze hounds. Greyhounds and Afghan hounds are descendants of the ancient Middle Eastern sight hounds.

As human society advanced, people began to tame the very animals they had once hunted. Sheep and goats were domesticated at the beginning of the Neolithic era, about 8000 B.C or 9000 B.C. By this time, people and dogs had been partners for several thousand years. Dogs were of great help to people in guarding and herding these new domestic animals. Ironically, one of the biggest threats to livestock was the dog's ancestor, the wolf. To protect their sheep and goats, shepherds needed dogs that were even larger and fiercer than wolves. So they began breeding giant dogs known as mastiffs. Mastiffs weighed as much as two hundred pounds, and were known for their courage and ferocity.

People also needed dogs to help herd the flocks. This was a job that dogs did particularly well. To understand why dogs were such good herders, we need to look back at one of the dog's wolflike behaviors. We saw earlier that a hunting strategy employed by wolves is to round up herds of animals, separate the weak or sick individuals from the flock, and attack these vulnerable animals.

This talent for rounding up animals was just what people

This guardian of the flock rescues a sheep from an attacking wolf.

needed to control flocks of sheep and goats. Of course, it would do a shepherd little good if his dogs herded the sheep and then ate them.

So once again, people solved their problem through selective breeding. To create a reliable herding dog, they selected dogs that would round up the sheep but stop short of attacking them. Collies and Shetland sheepdogs are among the modern dog breeds that continue to work as herders.

4

Guards, Hunters, and Pets

*T*he Neolithic era was a time of rapid change. It almost seemed as though humankind learned something new every day. Each new discovery helped people to survive a little more easily in their environment.

The development of more advanced tools was a big step, because it gave humans some control over their surroundings for the first time. Using polished stone axes, people were finally able to cut down trees to provide land for their villages and for farming.

Learning to grow and harvest crops was another important achievement during the Neolithic era. This advance occurred shortly after sheep and goats were domesticated. Now people had two reliable sources of food: the grains that they cultivated as well as the meat and milk from their livestock. With a steady food supply, people didn't have to worry as much about surviving from day to day. They could finally turn their attention to other things.

Using stone tools, they hollowed out tree trunks to form crude boats called dugouts. In these small boats they traveled by river

Guards, Hunters, and Pets

and sea to faraway places, trading goods with people from distant villages. In Europe, the Rhine and Danube rivers were important trade routes by which amber and other products from the north were transported to villages along the Mediterranean Sea.

Once again, new activities for people meant new opportunities for dogs. Travel was a dangerous business, and people needed dogs to protect them on their journeys, as well as to guard the villages while they were away. The big mastiffs that safeguarded the flocks were equally skilled at protecting people and their possessions. Years later, mastiffs were even used to help fight wars. These huge beasts, often wearing spiked metal collars, were trained to hurl themselves upon advancing troops. In classical

Dogs accompanied explorers on their travels, as this early woodcut shows.

Heavy leather armor protected canine soldiers on the battlefield. This suit of armor dates from the sixteenth century.

times, mastiffs wearing suits of armor helped their human allies by running through the battlefield and frightening the enemy's horses and elephants. Torches and knives mounted on their armor made these dogs of war even more fearsome.

As villages grew into cities, there came to be a need for smaller dogs to be kept as house pets. Mastiffs were useful as guard dogs, but they were altogether too big and cumbersome to have around the house. Small dogs that were docile and friendly with people were needed.

The silky white Maltese is one of the most ancient of the miniature, or "toy," breeds. Scientists believe that this breed descended from a polar dog that traveled south along the trade routes.

Toy dogs were very popular in Tibet, where people kept small, silken-haired dogs as companions. Our modern-day Shih Tzu and Lhasa apso breeds are descended from these early Tibetan house pets.

Chinese house dogs were little, pug-nosed animals known as *ha pa* ("under-table") dogs. Since Chinese tables in the early days were only about eight inches off the floor, *ha pa* dogs had to be very small indeed. It was from these dogs that the Pekingese breed was developed. These tiny dogs were sometimes carried in the sleeves of their masters' robes and so earned the name "sleeve dogs." Pekingese dogs had an almost mystical significance in China. They were the pampered pets of Chinese emperors and were treated with as much respect as their masters. The punishment for anyone caught smuggling a Pekingese out of the Imperial Palace was "death by a thousand cuts." All in all, the average Pekingese dog enjoyed a much more luxurious life than the average Chinese person.

Not all little dogs had it so easy. The terriers were a group of small dogs that had to work hard for their living. Terriers were bred to be hunters. But instead of going after big game, these small dogs specialized in small prey: the rats, weasels, and other pests that infested farms and villages. Terriers were (and still are) fearless animals. They will go to any lengths to catch their prey, even if that means following a fox or badger down into its den and dragging it to the surface. In fact, the name "terrier" comes from the Latin word *terra*, which means "earth." This is a reference to the terrier's willingness to "go to earth" in pursuit of its prey.

As time went by, different breeds of terrier were developed to hunt different types of animals. The medium-sized fox terrier specialized in hunting foxes, while the Manchester terrier was used to catch rats. Whatever their specialty, all terriers are courageous, love the chase, and, unlike many other dogs, do not hesitate to kill their prey.

Unfortunately, the terrier's aggressive and stubborn personality made it a natural choice for some of the more gruesome "sports" devised by people during medieval times.

One of these spectacles was bull baiting, and the dogs of choice were bulldogs and bull terriers. In a bull baiting competition, several dogs were pitted against a bull in a ring or in the village square. The method of attack was for a dog to bite the bull on the nose and hang on, no matter how violently the bull tossed it about. Interestingly, the nose-bite attack is a strategy sometimes used by wolves trying to bring down a moose. Though bull terriers differ in many ways from their wolf ancestors, nose biting is a behavior that they still share.

While bull baiting was eventually outlawed, another cruel sport, dogfighting, has continued to be popular (though illegal) to the present day. It should come as no surprise that the pit bull, the breed most commonly used for fighting, is a terrier.

As we've seen, dogs have been used for many purposes over the centuries—as scavengers, guards, herders, pest killers, and pets. But the dog's biggest role is the one for which it was first domesticated: to be man's partner in hunting. In fact, of the 131 dog breeds listed by the American Kennel Club, 55 are hunting dogs (sporting dogs and hounds).

In the early days, hunting was a necessity of life, since it (along with gathering fruits and nuts) was the only way for people to obtain food. As people learned to grow their own grain and vegetables and to get meat and milk from domesticated sheep, goats, and cattle, hunting became less important. It was no longer necessary to hunt in order to survive.

In this 2,500-year-old carving, Ashurbanipal, King of Assyria, hunts lions with nets and fierce mastiffs.

Instead of giving up hunting, man turned it into a sport. Humans are, after all, predators. Like terriers, some people enjoy the thrill of the chase as much as they enjoy what they catch. So people continued to hunt and to use dogs to help them catch their prey.

Over time, there came to be as many different kinds of hunting dog as there were animals to hunt. The kind and size of prey, as well as the features of the countryside—open land or dense forests—determined the type of dog that was required. As we saw earlier, speedy sight hounds were used to hunt gazelles on the flat, treeless plains of the Middle East. Another sight hound, the Irish wolfhound, was bred to chase wolves across the heaths of England and Ireland. The borzoi, or Russian wolfhound, did the same job on the steppes of Russia.

In heavily wooded country, hunters needed dogs that could track animals by smell. To fill this need, they selectively bred a large group of dogs whose talent was following their noses. These dogs, which ranged from bloodhounds and beagles (hounds) to spaniels and setters (sporting dogs), were all developed from the mastiff. Though they vary in size and shape, all scent-hunting dogs have the mastiff's floppy ears.

It would seem that a dog with floppy ears would be at a disadvantage—such a dog could never hear as well as a dog with pricked ears. But for a dog that hunts by scent, drooping ears might actually be useful, since they would screen out distracting sounds and let the dog concentrate on what its nose was telling it.

The scent hounds have traditionally been used to hunt in packs. In this kind of hunt, the hounds were released to pursue foxes or hares while hunters followed on horseback. The dogs barked continuously to indicate the direction they were heading. The hunters communicated with their dogs by means of hunting horns.

Guards, Hunters, and Pets 23

Different hounds were bred to chase different types of prey. Beagles and basset hounds went after hares and rabbits, coonhounds hunted raccoons, and foxhounds chased foxes. All of these breeds are related to the bloodhound, the most skillful scent hound known. Today's scent hounds work with customs agents and the

Hunters use horns to communicate with a pack of hounds as they pursue a stag.

Cocker spaniels were traditionally used to drive game out of the underbrush. Here, a modern-day spaniel leaps after its prey.

police to sniff out shipments of illegal drugs and to locate missing persons. Scent hounds can be trained to find almost anything by its smell. They have even been used to sniff out termites in peoples' houses!

While the hounds usually worked by themselves or in packs, another group of hunting dogs specialized in working one-on-one with their human partners. These were the sporting dogs: the spaniels, setters, pointers, and retrievers. Spaniels have been used for many centuries to find game, beginning in the days when birds were hunted with nets and trained hawks. These dogs worked either by dropping to the ground and holding the game until the hunters arrived or by flushing the game out of the underbrush into the talons of the hawks. The early "setting" spaniels were the ancestors of today's setters, while the "flushing" spaniels gave rise to our springer and cocker spaniels.

Like setters and spaniels, pointers have been helping people hunt for many years. Retrievers, on the other hand, came into being only after guns were perfected. With guns, hunters were able to shoot birds from far away, and they needed dogs to go after the fallen game and bring it back. Retrievers were bred and trained not only to retrieve the prey, but also to carry it gently to avoid damaging it. (After all, no hunter wanted to receive his bird with teeth marks all over it!) This last characteristic was known as a "soft mouth" and can still be seen in today's retrieving breeds.

Though each of the sporting breeds had its own special skill, there was one characteristic they all had in common: obedience to their human partners. A dog that captured and killed a hunter's prey would, after all, be more of a competitor than a helper. So sporting dogs were bred to assist people in finding and cornering their quarry, but to stop short of the actual kill—that was the privilege of the human hunter. In this respect, sporting dogs were very different from terriers. Though both were hunters, sporting dogs specialized in finding the prey, while terriers specialized in killing it.

Incredible as it may seem, all the dogs we've talked about—from the huge mastiff to the tiny Pekingese—are descended from one animal, the wolf. The various dog breeds look and act differently from one another because they have been "created" to perform different, specialized tasks. But underneath it all, every dog is still a wolf at heart.

Some of the behaviors we see in wolves can also be seen in every breed of domestic dog. Later on, we'll look more closely at the differences among breeds. But before we do, let's look at the thing all dogs have in common: their wolf ancestry. In the next section, we'll see that understanding the behavior of wolves can help us make sense of many of the things that all dogs do.

PART TWO

Wolves and Dogs

5

A Wolf Tale

*I*n the story of Little Red Riding Hood, the villain, a cunning and crafty wolf, meets a young girl in the forest. When he learns that she is on her way to her grandmother's house, he races ahead to arrive there first. After eating the old lady, the wolf disguises himself in her shawl and lies in wait for yet another tasty meal: Little Red Riding Hood.

The villain in *The Three Little Pigs* is also a wolf, one so fierce that he actually blows the pigs' houses down in order to capture them.

Throughout history, people have been afraid of wolves. Sometimes, this fear has been justified. Wolves are carnivores and will attack sheep, goats, and other domestic animals when their normal prey is scarce. More often, though, people were afraid of wolves because they didn't understand them. So they made up stories about imaginary wolves, which frightened them more than any real wolf could.

The legend of the werewolf, which was popular during the Middle Ages, held that certain people had the power to transform themselves into wolves. In this form, they would prowl at night, killing people and animals. Once their evil work was done, werewolves returned to their human shape. Like many other wolf tales, the legend of the werewolf shows this creature as a raving, bloodthirsty killer, with glowing eyes and huge, gleaming fangs.

In real life, the wolf is very different from the savage monster of our imaginations. In fact, many people are a little disappointed when they meet their first wolf. These animals are nowhere near as big or as ferocious-looking as people imagine them to be. More

This lone wolf looks more like a large dog than a bloodthirsty killer.

than anything else, a wolf resembles a rugged, thick-coated German shepherd or Alaskan malamute. Its teeth are generally not as big as people expect, but its feet are certainly bigger. The long, slender legs are built for running, something the wolf does a lot. Dense fur keeps the wolf warm in the coldest weather and repels water to keep it dry as well. By curling in a ball and covering its bare nose with the tip of its furry tail, a wolf can sleep comfortably even when the temperature drops to forty degrees below zero. (Wolflike dogs, such as huskies, also sleep this way in cold weather.)

Wolves survive by hunting other animals, and their bodies and minds are well adapted to this way of life. They are strong and can run fast and swim well. This allows them to go after animals both on land and in the water. Wolves have sensitive hearing, vision, and smell, and they use all three to track down their prey.

Above all, wolves are intelligent, able to change their hunting strategies to suit the behavior of the prey they are chasing. An animal that stands and fights, such as a bison, must be hunted in a different way than one whose best defense is running away. A solitary animal in the forest must be approached differently than a herd of animals on the open plains. As we shall see when we look at hunting dogs, people have taken advantage of this adaptability to create different breeds of dog that specialize in hunting different types of prey.

Wolves are adaptable in other ways as well. If moose or other large prey are not to be found, wolves will survive on rabbits, mice, or even insects. Because of their talent for adjusting to new situations, wolves have been able to thrive in all corners of the globe, from the snow-bound Arctic to the hot, dry Middle East, and almost everywhere in between.

Though they will eat just about anything if they have to, wolves prefer to eat meat. Large game such as moose, deer, and caribou are the major sources of meat in the wolf's diet. These animals are, for the most part, too big and too strong for one wolf to capture on its own. Even for a skilled hunter like the wolf, bringing down a thousand-pound moose requires teamwork. So it's not surprising that wolves hunt in groups.

Wolves are sociable animals. Even when they're not hunting, they live together in packs. A pack can be as small as two or three animals or as large as twenty animals. But whatever its size, a wolf pack is extremely well organized.

To understand why, let's look at the activity wolves do the most: hunting. In order to hunt successfully, wolves in a pack must cooperate. Like the players on a football team, each member of a wolf pack must know its job and work together with its teammates. If every wolf had a different idea of how the hunt should be conducted, the pack would never get anywhere and the wolves would go hungry.

WHY WOLVES COMMUNICATE

In order to carry out a hunting raid, settle a dispute, or just express affection, wolves must communicate with one another. In this way, they are like all social animals, including humans. (And dogs! As we look at some typical wolf behaviors, think about whether you have seen dogs showing the same behaviors.)

Wolves communicate with members of their own pack, as well as with neighboring packs. Much of the communication between wolves in the same pack is designed to keep the group together and reduce friction among individuals. Wolves communicate with other packs to define and defend their territory.

As we saw earlier, wolves have keen senses of hearing, vision, and smell. It's not surprising, then, that sounds, facial expressions and body postures (which are easy to see), and odors all play a role in wolf-to-wolf communication.

COMMUNICATING THROUGH SOUND

Let's look first at the kind of communication that is most familiar to people: sounds. Wolves in the wild make many different sounds, but the most famous is certainly the howl. Wolves howl when they are together and also when they are by themselves. Some of the reasons for howling are to sound an alarm, to get the pack together before a hunt, and to locate each other when they are separated. Some scientists think that a lone, howling wolf is saying, "Here I am! Where is the rest of my pack?" As most dog owners (and neighbors of dog owners) know, dogs may also resort to howling when they are left at home alone. They are probably calling out to the missing members of their human pack.

Barking is a much less important behavior for wolves than it is for dogs. Wolves do not bark very often and, when they do, the sound is very soft and quiet. Because of this, it was a long time before people realized that wolves barked at all!

Different as it sounds, the wolf's bark serves the same purpose as the dog's bark: to sound a warning to the pack. Both wolves and dogs bark when an intruder enters their territory. For wolves, this is the area immediately around the den, while for dogs, it is the house and yard of the human "pack." Dogs bark louder and more often than wolves because people have selectively bred their dogs for this behavior.

Another sound that both wolves and dogs make is a growl. To anyone who has been on the receiving end of a dog's low, deep-throated growl, the message is clear: watch out! Wolves and dogs growl when they are angry and about to attack, when they are fighting over a piece of food, and when they want to threaten or assert their authority over another animal.

COMMUNICATING THROUGH BODY LANGUAGE

When a wolf threatens another animal, it doesn't just growl. Its whole body gets into the act. Why? Because, for its threat to be taken seriously, it's not enough for a wolf to *sound* aggressive. It also needs to *look* as big and as menacing as possible. So it stands tall, with legs stiff and brushlike tail held high. Its hackles—the hairs along the shoulders and back—are raised, making its body look larger than it really is. Its ears are erect and pointed forward, its teeth are bared, and its glaring eyes are narrowed to slits. From deep in its throat comes the familiar, rumbling growl.

It's easy to see how this wolf's body language helps it get its message across. If it's lucky, another wolf that sees this threat will decide that the threatening wolf is too dangerous and will give up. The threatening wolf will have established its authority without having to fight for it.

Within the pack, the alpha wolves often threaten other members of the pack in this way. Their intention is not to start a fight. It is simply to remind the other animals who is boss. The threat display becomes a kind of ritual that the alpha wolf performs to maintain its authority over the group.

When a lower-ranking member of the pack is threatened by a dominant wolf, the response is dramatic. Even more than the dominant wolf, the weaker animal wants to avoid a fight (because it will probably end up the loser). So the weaker wolf has a ritual of its own, designed to reassure the alpha wolf that it knows its place and means no harm. In this ritual, called passive submission, the weaker wolf tries to act as nonaggressive as possible. In fact, everything it does is just the opposite of what the threatening wolf is doing. While the dominant wolf stands tall, the submissive wolf crouches low, or even rolls on its back. Its paws hang limply, its tail is tucked between its legs, and its ears are flattened back along its head. While the dominant wolf bares its teeth, the submissive wolf pulls its lips back into a sort of grin that partially hides its teeth. (This grin looks quite a bit like a human smile, and has a similar meaning. A smile, whether it comes from a person, a wolf, or a dog, says, "I'm friendly, not a threat. Don't attack me.")

In response to the alpha wolf's penetrating stare, the submissive wolf looks away or flashes the whites of its eyes. And instead of growling, it whimpers and whines like a puppy. (In fact, all these behaviors are like those of a helpless puppy.) Passive submission is the wolf's way of waving a white flag, of saying, "I know you're the top dog, and I'm not going to challenge you." It is a ritual that the dominant wolf understands perfectly. After growling a bit more, it usually backs off and allows the submissive animal to slink away unharmed.

Passive submission is an extreme response to a threat by a dominant wolf. Sometimes, low-ranking wolves want to reassure the leader that they know who's boss, even though it hasn't challenged them. To do this, the subordinate wolf resorts to another puppylike ritual, called active submission. Active submission is the kind of friendly greeting behavior that dogs often show their human masters.

Some of the behaviors are the same as those seen in passive submission, designed to make the animal appear small and nonthreatening. The submissive wolf crouches down so that it is looking up at the leader. Its ears are flattened and its lips are pulled back in a submissive grin. While wagging its tail, the low-ranking wolf approaches the alpha animal and tries to lick and nuzzle its face. This ritual probably has its roots in the food-begging behavior that wolf pups show when their parents return to the den.

In order to provide enough food for their growing pups, wolf parents must hunt every day. After making a kill, they gobble down the meat themselves. When the wolves return to the den, they are greeted by the excited pups, who lick their parents' faces. This behavior stimulates the adults to regurgitate the food that they have brought back, so the pups can eat.

Body language is one of the most important ways that wolves have of communicating among themselves. Rituals such as threat, active submission, and passive submission are used to make sure every wolf knows its place in the pack. If they seem familiar, it is because domestic dogs, considering humans to be members of their pack, show these behaviors all the time.

Dog owners who have trained their pets well see mostly the friendly, submissive behaviors. A well-trained dog thinks of its human owners as the alpha members of the pack and depends on them for guidance and direction. Just as a low-ranking wolf wants to please the alpha animal, most dogs want to please their owners. The face-licking, tail-wagging greeting your dog gives you is, in reality, the active submission ritual. It's your dog's way of saying, "You're the boss and I'll do anything you say." When it's done something wrong, the same dog may tuck its tail between its legs and go belly up. It may not know *why* you're angry, but it knows it had better respond submissively to your scolding "threat display."

People who are not so lucky, or who are not such good dog trainers, may end up with a dog that thinks it is the pack leader. And it tries to prove it all the time by growling, snapping, and generally refusing to do what it's told. Why should it give in to a pack member it considers inferior, even if that pack member is a human?

COMMUNICATING THROUGH SMELL

Important as sounds and body language may be, they're not the whole story when it comes to canine communication. Wolves and dogs have a keen sense of smell, and odors play a much bigger part in their lives than they do in ours.

When two wolves meet, they investigate each other with their noses. If the wolves are friends, they will usually sniff each other's faces, head, and neck. When a dominant wolf meets a subordinate, it tries to sniff underneath the subordinate wolf's tail. The low-ranking wolf often reacts by putting its tail between its legs, perhaps trying to hide its identity from the dominant animal.

Because we don't depend on odors to communicate, it seems strange that an animal can find out who someone is by that person's smell. But that's exactly what wolves and dogs do. This is why a dog insists on sniffing your hand (or other, more embarrassing, places) when it meets you. Your special smell lets it know who you are.

Wolves also use odors to leave messages for other wolves, through a ritual known as scent marking. Anyone who has seen a male dog out for a walk will recognize this behavior. After selecting and sniffing a conspicuous scent post, such as a rock or tree stump, the animal lifts his leg and squirts a few drops of urine on the spot. Sometimes he scratches the ground after marking, probably to leave a visual message to go along with the odor. Scent marking has nothing to do with having to relieve himself. A dog may continue to lift his leg at scent posts even when his bladder is empty.

Scientists are not sure whether scent messages are intended for members of a wolf's own pack or for wolves in other packs. It could be that they serve both purposes, with the meaning of the message changing depending upon who "reads" it. Members of a pack might use scent marks to create a map of their territory and to communicate when they are separated. The same scent marks might warn wolves in other packs to stay away.

HUNTING

We've seen that wolves have a sophisticated system of communication based on sounds, body postures, and odors. Howling, leg lifting, and a variety of other behaviors are all ways of sending a message to other animals. But wolves do other things besides communicate. The wolf is, first and foremost, a predator, and many of its activities are related to finding, capturing, and eating prey animals. This takes more time than one might imagine: The average wolf spends nearly one-third of its life hunting!

With their sharp senses and strong, fast bodies, wolves are built to hunt. One of the myths about wolves is that they can make a kill whenever they want to. This is probably true when it comes to easy prey such as domestic sheep and cattle. These animals are not accustomed to running away, and, even if they were, they usually have nowhere to run. In the wild, however, the wolf and its prey are much more evenly matched. Just as the wolf has developed strategies for hunting moose, deer, and caribou, these animals have developed strategies for eluding an attack. In fact, they are often better at escaping than the wolves are at catching them. In a study of wolves in Isle Royale, Michigan, a wildlife biologist named David Mech watched encounters between wolves and moose. Out of seventy-seven confrontations, the wolves managed to kill only six animals—the other seventy-one got away.

Hunting is by no means an easy task for wolves. They have to "test" many animals before finding one they can catch. Unless they run into them by accident, wolves must start out by locating their prey. This they usually do by smell—either by sniffing the air to catch the scent of a prey animal or by following a fresh track on the ground. (The wolf's ability to track by scent has been intensified in some breeds of hunting dog, most notably the bloodhound. Over generations of selective breeding, smell has become the most important sense for these dogs. As a result, they have an even keener sense of smell than their wolf ancestors.)

Once they have found a prey animal, the wolves creep slowly and quietly toward it. They stalk so silently that they can often get very close to their quarry before being spotted. The moment of truth comes when the hunted animal senses the wolves' approach. When this happens, the wolves freeze in their tracks. Predator and prey stand motionless, sizing each other up. The wolves look for any signs of age or illness that would make the prey an easier target. The prey animal notes the number of wolves and their distance. Eventually, the prey must decide whether to stand its ground or flee. Surprisingly, an animal that doesn't try to run sometimes has a better chance of surviving. This is especially true for moose and elk, which are large enough to fight back. By standing still, the animal may be telling the wolves, "Don't bother attacking, because you're not going to win." When this happens, the wolves often give up and go on to look for easier prey.

If the prey does decide to run, the wolves almost always pursue and try to attack. The sight of a fleeing animal seems irresistible to wolves—they just have to go after it. This behavior is known as the chase response and it can be seen in dogs as well as wolves. A motionless animal seems to stop the chase response, while an animal running away triggers it. The chase response is especially well developed in sight-hunting dogs such as greyhounds and salukis.

Knowing about the chase response can help you if you are ever confronted by an unfriendly dog. Standing still is your best bet, because it tells the dog you are not afraid—even if you are. If you show weakness by running, the dog will almost certainly chase and try to bite you.

When the prey is a herd animal such as reindeer or caribou, wolves use a different approach. Unlike the moose, which may fight back, these animals survive by running away. The successful ones are those that outrun the wolves.

Wolves hunt caribou and reindeer by chasing the entire herd and watching for old or weak animals that cannot keep up with the rest of the group. When these animals fall behind, they are singled out and attacked. Wolf packs have also been seen herding groups of caribou toward a waiting wolf. These were the behaviors (minus the attack, of course) that people selected when they created herding dogs.

EATING

Once a pack of wolves has killed a moose or caribou, they devour it hungrily. Like dogs, wolves always seem to be hungry, and they can consume huge quantities of food at one time. Biologist David Mech tells of a wolf pack that ate an entire moose in less than two hours! Before too long the pack was out again hunting for more food.

Most dog owners have noticed this trait in their pets. Not only will dogs eat almost anything, they are always ready to eat.

The reason for this behavior is the "feast or famine" nature of the wolf's existence. Like all animals that hunt for a living, wolves never know when—or if—they will get their next meal. If prey animals are scarce, a wolf pack may be forced to go for several days or a week without eating. But they make up for it when they catch something by gorging themselves until they can barely move.

Not only do wolves eat a lot, they eat quickly. If you've ever seen a dog gulp down its dinner, you'll recognize this trait. Wolves and many dogs are possessive about their food, and will growl and snap at anyone who approaches while they are eating.

In the wild, these behaviors—"wolfing" down food and guarding it jealously—help these predators to survive. When wolves are lucky, they may bring down an adult moose that is large enough to feed the whole pack. But sometimes the prey animal is not so big, and there isn't enough to go around. To get its share, a wolf must dive right in, eating as much and as fast as it can, and threatening any animal that gets in the way. These behaviors are so deeply ingrained that they can often be seen even in domestic dogs that have plenty to eat.

On the rare occasions when there is more food than the wolves can eat, they may dig a hole and bury some for later. The advantage of burying extra food is that the covering of cool earth refrigerates it and keeps flies away. Wolves sometimes return to dig up the food they have hidden, but, more often, they forget about it. Like a dog with a bone, the wolf seems to consider the act of burying the food the important thing.

In this chapter, we've learned about a variety of wolf behaviors. Though some may seem mysterious, most of these behaviors are ones we see every day in our domestic dogs. Unfortunately, acting like a wolf can sometimes get a dog into trouble. As we'll see in the next chapter, howling, chewing, and other "dog problems" can often be explained by our pets' wolf heritage.

6

Wolf in Dog's Clothing: Understanding Your Pet's Behavior

Studying the habits of wolves in the wild can help us understand many of the behaviors we see in domestic dogs. Two characteristics are particularly important: the wolf's sociable, pack-living nature and its impulse to hunt.

Sociability is probably the wolf's most striking feature. In fact, it was this trait that enabled people to domesticate wolves in the first place. Their history as social animals explains why dogs bark, wag their tails, and lift their legs. Their hunting ancestry tells us why they wolf down their food and bury bones.

Most of these behaviors are ones we like, or at least ones we can tolerate. But the dog's wolf heritage can also cause some difficulties, especially when we ask this animal to adjust to human society—one that is very different from its own.

Because dogs are social animals, major problems can arise when we ignore their need for companionship. Wolves in the wild spend most of their days in the company of other wolves. Hunting, eating, playing, and sleeping are all group activities. Dogs, on the

Greeting is an important canine ritual. Here, one dog strains at its leash to sniff a passerby.

other hand, are frequently abandoned for long periods of time by their human pack. Mom and Dad work, the kids are in school, and the dog stays home alone all day.

Being alone is not something the average dog enjoys. Separated from its pack, it becomes lonely, frightened, and nervous. Where did they go? When are they coming back? Are they coming back at all? And what if something terrible happens while they're gone? First, the dog may bark and howl in an attempt to locate its lost pack members. When they don't answer, its howls grow louder and longer. As many dog owners know, these plaintive cries may go on for quite some time. Unfortunately, they seldom have any effect, other than disturbing the neighbors.

Getting more agitated by the minute, the dog looks around for another way to relieve its anxiety. If it were human, it might bite its nails or pace back and forth or wring its hands. But, being a dog, it does what dogs do when they are nervous: It chews. It doesn't matter if the object is a pair of socks, the bathroom rug, or the living-room couch—as long as the dog can sink its teeth into something, it feels a little better. If it can find an object whose smell reminds it of its missing pack, it's even more comforting. That's why your dog always seems to choose your favorite socks, sweater, or scarf to destroy while you are away from home. It's not doing it because it's angry. It's just that your favorite things— the ones you use the most—smell more like you than anything else your dog can find.

When left alone, some dogs relieve anxiety by chewing on shoes and other objects.

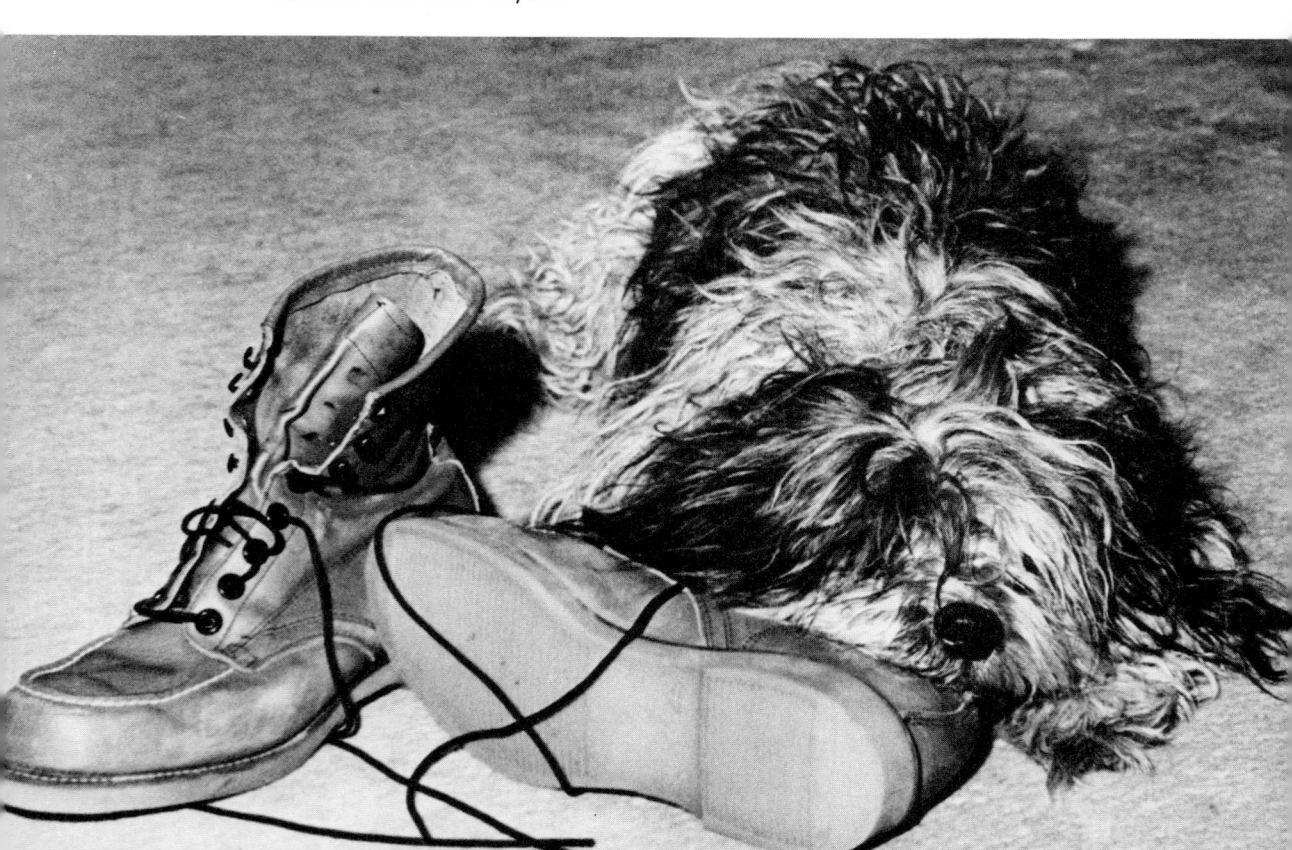

Another thing that makes a dog edgy when it is home alone is the heavy responsibility of protecting its territory. It may not be the top dog when its pack is there but, when they are gone, it feels it has been left in charge. As a result, it is extra alert for sounds that might signal an intruder. The mail carrier on the porch, someone passing by the apartment door—either one could be a trespasser. So the dog does what any self-respecting den protector would do: It barks. Some dogs bark only when the danger is real. But others go overboard, barking at the slightest noise, real or imaginary. Like the dog that howls when its pack is gone, the overzealous watchdog can be quite an annoyance to the next-door neighbors.

This dog can be an annoyance to its pack, too, when they get home. For, in addition to barking, the dog may have protected its turf in another way: by marking its territory. According to some dog trainers, this is most likely to happen when the dog cannot do anything about the noises it hears. Either they don't stop when the dog barks or it can't look out a window to see what is causing them. So the dog lifts its leg to send an odor message to would-be intruders: "I'm in charge here. Keep out of my territory!" Though the dog means well, its family will almost certainly not appreciate its efforts when they return home. (Sometimes, of course, a dog leaves its family a little "gift" for other reasons. It could be that it is not completely housetrained, and has been left alone too long. Or perhaps the dog does not have a strong human pack leader. Dogs that are not very dominant often become anxious when they do not have a strong leader, and soil the house as a result.)

The best way to avoid these problems is to take your dog along with you when you go out. The next best thing is to make its stay at home a less frightening experience. To calm its fear of being left alone, you must let it know that you will always come back. One way to do this is to go away at first only for very short times—five or ten minutes at the most. As the dog learns to survive these separations without howling, you can gradually go away for longer and longer periods of time.

To reduce your dog's nervousness about having to guard the whole house, it helps to give it a miniature den inside your home. (Many dog trainers recommend a wire kennel crate like those used at dog shows.) The "miniden" has several advantages: It is a smaller territory to protect, so the dog won't become as agitated and probably won't bark as much. If it does get jumpy, despite everything you've done, it will be able to take it out on the chew toy you have left inside the crate, rather than on your favorite shirt. And finally, because dogs have a rule against soiling the place where they sleep, it is much less likely to have an accident or mark its territory inside its little den. (If you do use a crate, be sure not to leave your dog in it for more than a couple of hours at a stretch. For puppies, the crate time should be even shorter.)

As we just saw, canine "misbehaviors" such as howling, barking, and chewing often occur when a dog is separated from its pack. Growling, biting, and refusing to obey are also related to the pack, but in a slightly different way. A dog that shows these behaviors usually believes it is the dominant member of its pack. As a result, it acts just like an alpha wolf, using threats and intimidation to control its packmates. If you have a dog you can't control, it is very important to get help right away. A trainer who specializes in dominant or aggressive dogs should be able to help you raise your status in your pet's eyes.

While some problem behaviors stem from the dog's history as a pack animal, others can be traced to its history as a hunter. We saw how wolves test their prey for signs of weakness, chasing and attacking those animals that flee. Remnants of these behaviors still exist in domestic dogs. They explain why some dogs threaten people on the street (the test) and why they run after cats, cars, joggers, and anything else that tries to get away (the chase). These are natural behaviors for dogs, but they are real problems for the people involved. They can end up getting the dogs into trouble, too—many are hurt or killed each year while chasing cars. A dog trainer can help break your dog's chasing habit, but the best way to solve this problem is to prevent it by keeping your pet in a fenced yard or on a leash.

A dog that growls and snaps at people who come near its food bowl is showing another natural canine behavior. This behavior is important for wolves in the wild, because it helps them get enough to eat. But when domestic dogs do the same thing, it is annoying and sometimes dangerous to their human packmates.

Like all the problems we have talked about, this one can usually be solved. The first step is understanding why the dog acts the way it does. Sometimes this knowledge will be all you need to change or prevent the behavior. At other times, you may require help, either from a professional dog trainer or from one of the many good books on dog training.

In this chapter, we have seen that some of the things dogs do are not nearly so mysterious when we understand the behavior of wolves. Because all dogs belong to the same species, *Canis familiaris,* which is descended from the wolf, all dogs have certain wolflike characteristics.

Within this one species, however, there are over one hundred distinct breeds of dog. As anyone knows, the variety among the different breeds is enormous. When we compare an alert, protective German shepherd with a sluggish basset hound, it is hard to believe that they are so closely related. Sometimes it seems that the *only* thing they share is their wolf heritage.

The various breeds of dog diverged from their original wolf ancestors, and from each other, because they were deliberately bred to assist people in different ways. In the next section, we'll take a closer look at the jobs dogs have been bred to do, and we'll see how these have helped to shape each breed's looks and behavior.

PART THREE

Why Is a Dachshund Different from a Doberman?

7

Picking the Right Dog

Next time you go to the park, see how many different kinds of dogs you can spot. Chances are, you'll see an incredible array, from big, shaggy sheepdogs to petite poodles to medium-sized mutts. If you watch closely, you'll notice that these dogs don't just look different from one another, they act differently, too. Some are outgoing and friendly while others are aloof or downright aggressive. Some are bundles of energy while others are content to sleep on the grass. If you were to question the people at the other end of the leashes, they all would probably say that their particular breed makes a great pet.

And it's true—all breeds of dog can make good pets, provided they are matched up with the right kinds of people. But if the dog you choose doesn't fit your life-style, the results can be disastrous.

How can you tell what breed of dog is best for you? Some people decide what they want their dog to look like (cute and cuddly, tough and aggressive, sleek and elegant) and make the choice that way. But looks aren't everything. What's on the inside—a dog's temperament—is just as important as what it looks like.

While it is impossible to predict the way any individual dog will behave, there are certain characteristics that are more common in some breeds than in others. For example, a high activity level is more common in Afghan hounds than it is in bulldogs.

Why is this? Quite simply, because Afghan hounds were originally bred to run after swift game while bulldogs were not. Even though most modern-day Afghans do not hunt, they still have the desire to run and the speed of their hunting ancestors. Knowing this breed's history (or the history of any other breed) can help you decide which dog is right for you.

8

Hard Labor: The Working Breeds

Long before they became pets, dogs were bred to work. The American Kennel Club, an organization that recognizes and registers dog breeds in the United States, now classifies nineteen breeds as working dogs. Over the years, working dogs have done many jobs, including hauling sleds, guarding people and property, and rescuing stranded travelers. As one might expect from dogs with such diverse backgrounds, the variety among the working breeds is tremendous. For instance, the Great Dane and the Samoyed look nothing alike, yet they are both working dogs. The one thing common to almost all of these breeds is their size. With few exceptions, they are large, powerful animals, built to work hard.

Among the oldest working dogs are those from the polar regions: the Siberian husky, the Samoyed, and the Alaskan malamute. These breeds have been helping people to survive in a cold, hostile environment for thousands of years.

The nomadic tribes that inhabited these regions first used their dogs to hunt the reindeer that roamed the tundra. Because they depended upon reindeer for survival, people spent their lives fol-

With their pointed muzzles and thick fur, polar breeds such as this Samoyed closely resemble their wolf ancestors.

lowing the herds. They soon discovered that the dogs could help them by hauling sleds loaded with their possessions. Early sleds were fashioned of whalebone or driftwood with baskets made of seal or walrus hide. Sometimes reindeer antlers were lashed to the sled to serve as handlebars. When fully loaded, the sleds were very heavy and it required a team of strong dogs to pull one.

Even after the nomads settled down, they traveled from one village to another by dog sled. In fact, until the snowmobile was invented, sled dogs were the most important means of transportation in the frozen north.

The polar regions were home to many nomadic tribes, and each one had a slightly different version of the basic polar dog. These different strains would later develop into the distinct breeds we know today. The Chukchi people of Siberia bred a wolflike dog that was an ancestor of the Siberian husky. Another tribe from Siberia, the Samoyeds, used their large white dogs to herd reindeer as well as to pull sleds. And guess what breed originated with the Mahlemut (or Malamute) people of northern Alaska?

During the 1800s any dog that pulled a sled was called a husky. This name was a variation of the word *esky*, a slang term for Eskimo. Though huskies were essential to survival for people in the north, they were little known in other parts of the world. It was not until the great Alaskan Gold Rush at the turn of the century that attention was finally focused on these dogs. It was then that dog teams became an important means of transportation not just for the natives but for the hordes of prospectors who flocked to Alaska to seek their fortunes.

In 1908 the first All-Alaska Sweepstakes was held. This grueling sled-dog race covered a 408-mile course over rough terrain and offered a prize of $10,000 to the winner. As the sport of sled-dog racing grew in popularity, people began to take an interest in the polar breeds. In 1906 the Samoyed was first registered by the American Kennel Club, followed by the Siberian husky in 1930 and the Alaskan malamute in 1935.

More than most other dogs, the northern breeds look like their wolf ancestors. With their pricked ears, pointed muzzles, bushy tails, and dense fur, the resemblance to wolves is striking. These dogs sometimes act a bit like wolves as well. Siberian huskies, for instance, bark much less than many other breeds. When they do make noise, it is more likely to be a howl.

Centuries of work as draft animals have also affected the looks and behavior of these breeds. Sled dogs were expected not only to haul heavy loads, but to keep going for long distances without getting tired. They were expected to work despite subfreezing temperatures and blinding snowstorms. To be successful, a sled dog needed incredible energy and amazing resistance to the cold.

Pulling sleds is a thing of the past for most polar dogs, but the qualities that made them superior draft animals are still there. If you choose a husky, Samoyed, or malamute as a pet, be prepared to give it lots of exercise. These dogs never seem to get tired. Because of this, they will become very restless if kept in a small house or apartment.

Their thick, fluffy coats look beautiful and keep these dogs warm in the coldest weather. But, like most long-haired dogs, polar dogs shed a great deal. Even if you brush your pet every day, you will probably have a house full of hair.

Perhaps because they look so much like wolves, the polar breeds are sometimes thought to be unfriendly or vicious. In reality, nothing could be further from the truth. Though they may be competitive with other dogs, they usually get along quite well with people. This makes sense when you think about their history. The polar breeds were never used to guard or attack, so there was no reason to select for an aggressive or fierce personality. These dogs are a great choice if you want a pet that will get along with the family. If you are looking for a guard dog, you should choose another breed.

Though polar dogs love people, they occasionally fight with other dogs. Conflicts are especially likely to occur between males or between dogs that are dominant. As with other behaviors, we can understand this by looking back at the polar dogs' history as sled dogs. A working sled-dog team is, in many ways, like a wolf pack. One dog is always the leader, and it is he (or sometimes she) who sets the pace and encourages the others to keep running. To become team leader—or even to get enough to eat—sled dogs must compete with each other. This competition often results in squabbles. Although few of today's polar dogs work in teams, the tendency to fight is still there.

Like an alpha wolf, the lead sled dog is boss, and all the other dogs in the team look to him or her for direction. On the trail, sled dogs are much more likely to pay attention to the lead dog than to the person driving the sled. Because of this characteristic, the polar breeds are not always the easiest dogs to train. It is not that they are stupid—they are simply not used to taking orders from people. Firm and patient training is the key to success with these breeds.

Because of their strong pack instinct, the polar breeds are usually happiest in the company of other dogs. When left alone, they become nervous and restless. Whining, howling, and destructive chewing are sometimes the results. If you can manage it, consider getting two of these dogs to keep each other company. To decrease the likelihood of fighting, it is best to pick littermates that have grown up together. Two females or a male and a female will not be as apt to fight as two males. There will also be less friction if you have your pets spayed or neutered. This is always a good idea, and if you have a male and a female, it is essential.

Except for the polar dogs, most modern working breeds are descended from the ancient mastiffs. Today there is a single breed known as the mastiff, but in the past the word was used to describe a whole group of gigantic, ferocious dogs. The history of these dogs goes back thousands of years. Egyptian drawings from the year 3000 B.C. show large mastifflike dogs. When Caesar invaded Britain in 55 B.C. he wrote of the huge fighting dogs he encountered. Soon afterward, mastiffs were brought back to Rome, where they were pitted against bulls, lions, and even human gladiators. Mastiffs have also fought alongside soldiers in wartime.

One of the first peaceful uses to which these big dogs were put was guarding flocks of sheep against wild animals. Good grazing land was often found on remote hillsides, surrounded by forests. A flock of sheep was always in danger of being attacked by a wolf or bear. To watch over their flocks, shepherds used big dogs outfitted with spiked metal collars. These dogs were usually white, so that they blended in with the sheep they were guarding. A white coat was thought to be less frightening to the sheep, and it had the added advantage of turning the dog into an undercover agent: A wolf creeping up on an unsuspecting flock could never be sure when one of the "sheep" would suddenly attack.

Two of these early sheep-guarding breeds are the Great Pyrenees, from the mountains between France and Spain, and the komondor, from Hungary. Both are pure white, with long, thick

The komondor's shaggy, white coat made it difficult to distinguish from the sheep it guarded.

coats to protect them from the cold. Because they have worked alone for so many years, they are very independent.

As time went on, people found that dogs were as good at guarding people and their property as they were at guarding sheep. One of the oldest guarding breeds, the rottweiler, actually started out herding livestock.

A mastifflike ancestor of the rottweiler was first used by the Roman legions to drive cattle. During the first century A.D., the Roman army advanced over the Alps into an area that is now Germany. Huge quantities of meat were required to feed the troops, and the easiest way to transport it was "on the hoof." Dogs were needed to drive the cattle by day and to guard them by night. The Roman troops finally settled in southern Germany. One of their camps grew into the city of Rottweil, which later became a major cattle-trading center.

The Roman cattle dogs had their work cut out for them. In addition to driving cattle to market, the dogs acted as bodyguards for farmers returning home with money from the sale of their livestock. By placing the money in a leather pouch and tying the pouch around his dog's neck, a farmer could be assured of a safe trip home. Even armed bandits were reluctant to tangle with a big, protective rottweiler.

Another guarding breed, the bullmastiff, was developed many centuries later for a very specific task. In nineteenth-century England the problem of game poaching on big estates was severe. Gamekeepers had a hard time stopping the poachers, who would do anything—including killing the gamekeeper—to avoid being captured. They needed a dog that could overpower and hold a poacher until the authorities arrived. In the late 1800s the bullmastiff (also known as the gamekeeper's night dog) was created by crossing a mastiff with a bulldog. The bullmastiff has the mastiff's size along with the bulldog's tenacity and aggressiveness. This breed is just as effective in stopping prowlers today as it was in stopping poachers a hundred years ago.

One of the best-known guard dogs, the Doberman pinscher, was created by a man named Ludwig Dobermann in the late 1800s. Dobermann was, among other things, a nighttime police officer, and he wanted a dog to protect him. The Doberman's ancestors include the rottweiler and the black-and-tan terrier (in fact, *pinscher* is the German word for "terrier"). Its terrier ancestry explains why the Doberman is thinner, lighter, and more active than the other mastifflike guard dogs.

Dobermans are often thought to be naturally fierce and aggressive. This belief comes in part from their use in World War II, where they were known as devil dogs. It also comes from their appearance. Cropped ears and a docked tail make the Doberman look more ferocious than it really is. In Britain, where ear cropping and tail docking are rarely done, Dobermans appear much less threatening.

Because of their large size, all the mastifflike dogs make good guards. One that had an additional job was the Great Dane. During the Middle Ages, this breed was used to hunt the fierce and dangerous wild boar. The Great Dane was the only dog big, strong, and fast enough for the job. The ears of these dogs were originally cropped so that they would not be ripped by the fighting boar. Some Great Dane owners still crop their pets' ears, perhaps to give these huge dogs a more menacing appearance.

Though most of the working breeds were guard dogs, two breeds were developed for a very specialized purpose: rescuing people. The Saint Bernard was first brought to the hospice of Saint Bernard during the 1600s to serve as a watchdog and draft animal. The hospice, located eight thousand feet above sea level

Despite their massive size and occasionally threatening appearance, both the Great Dane (above) and the Saint Bernard (below) can be gentle and friendly family pets.

in the Swiss Alps, was near the mountain pass connecting Switzerland and Italy. The weather at this altitude was always bad and the pass was frequently snowed in. It was common for travelers to become lost or trapped by avalanches. The monks of the hospice began taking their dogs along to search for lost travelers and were astonished at the dogs' ability to find people by scent. Soon they started breeding dogs just for this purpose and the Saint Bernards became famous for their skill at locating people trapped underneath the snow. The best-known Saint Bernard was Barry, who rescued forty people during his lifetime.

The Newfoundland is also known as a rescue dog, but this breed's specialty is water rescue. The origins of the breed are unclear. Some say its ancestor was the Great Pyrenees, brought to the island of Newfoundland by Basque fishermen. Others think that the black Labrador retriever (which actually came from Newfoundland) was the ancestor of the breed. Whatever their history, these dogs are perfectly suited to life near the water. As you might expect, they love to swim. Their fur is dense and oily to repel water and keep them warm. Unlike other dogs, Newfoundlands have webbed feet, which help them move through the water with ease.

Over the years, Newfoundlands have helped fishermen by plunging into the sea and pulling in nets full of fish. They have also saved hundreds of shipwreck victims from drowning.

Like Saint Bernards, Newfoundlands are surprisingly gentle and friendly for their size. Because they were not designed to be guards, these two breeds are a bit less aggressive than some of the other working dogs. Even though they are easygoing, their size alone is enough to frighten away intruders.

Many people hesitate to get one of the working breeds as a pet because they assume these big dogs need a tremendous amount of exercise. As we saw, the polar breeds do need lots of activity to keep them happy. But most of the guarding breeds, despite their large size, are fairly placid. When you consider their job, it's easy to see why.

Guarding is a job that can, for the most part, be done sitting down. Occasionally a guard dog must get up to look around or chase an intruder, but the rest of the time it sits, waiting patiently for something to happen. The ability to sit and wait is a trait that many of the large dogs share, and it makes them easier pets than one might expect. (Of course, like all dogs, these large breeds need exercise.)

Being a guard is also a solitary job. Guard dogs, especially the mountain breeds that protected flocks of sheep, have traditionally spent a lot of time by themselves. As a result, they are more accustomed to being alone than some other breeds are.

To do guard or rescue work, a dog must be dependable. It must also be able to make its own decisions. These breeds are very dependable and very independent. Rather than look to a person for instructions, they are more likely to do what they think is right. This can be frustrating, especially when you want the dog to do one thing and it wants to do another.

Because of their guarding background, most of the working breeds are somewhat aggressive and dominant. These traits, combined with their independence and their size, can make these dogs a real handful. If this type of dog thinks of you as submissive, it will probably never obey, and may even threaten or challenge you. If your four-pound Chihuahua showed this behavior, you might overlook it or even think it was cute. But a challenge from a hundred-pound rottweiler is no joke. It is important that these dogs see you as boss. The way to accomplish this is through gentle, but consistent, obedience training.

Though they can be aggressive at times, these dogs are not likely to bite or attack without warning. As guards, their job was to frighten off wild animals and human intruders. If they could do that without a fight, so much the better. Because of this, guard dogs put on a very threatening act. They raise their hackles, growl, and bark fiercely to let their opponents know they are serious about attacking. A guard dog may eventually bite you, but it is likely to give you some warning first. Other dogs, such as the terriers we'll meet later, are more likely to take you by surprise.

Something you should consider if you want a working dog is its appetite. Most big dogs are big eaters, so before you get your new pet, be sure you can afford to feed it.

9

Bringing in the Sheep: The Herding Breeds

*E*ver since people first domesticated sheep, goats, and cattle, they have relied on dogs to help manage their flocks. In the earliest days, dogs were used mainly as guards. As we saw earlier, the Great Pyrenees and the komondor were two breeds that had their origins as guardians of the flocks.

As time went on, many of the forests were cleared to make room for farms, and the wild forest animals were wiped out by hunters. The wolf, for instance, has been extinct in the British Isles for several hundred years (due, in part, to a dog we'll meet later, the Irish wolfhound). As wolves and other predators disappeared, the role of flock-protecting dogs became less important. Except in remote areas, it was no longer necessary to have a big dog standing guard.

More open land meant that more space could be used for grazing sheep and cattle. Shepherds could begin to keep larger flocks. But the bigger the flocks became the harder they were to control. A shepherd who could easily manage five or ten sheep found that he needed help when his flock grew to several hundred. The ideal assistant was a quicker, more agile dog that could keep the flock together and help the shepherd move his animals from place to place. The large working dogs were too slow to be very good at this, and they preferred sitting in one spot all day to running after a flock of sheep. So people began to breed smaller, more active dogs. These dogs learned quickly, obeyed their masters' commands, and could be trusted around the livestock.

Though guarding was not their main job, they were still very protective. Some of the larger breeds, such as the Old English sheepdog and the briard, did both jobs at once, herding the flocks while at the same time protecting them against wild animals.

The way most herding dogs worked (and still work today) was to circle around a group of animals, barking and nipping at their heels to move them along. Though the dogs snapped at their charges, they never really bit them very hard. And it was a good thing they didn't! A herding dog that injured or attacked the animals in its care was certainly no help to the shepherd. To

A herding dog rounds up its flock. White markings on tail, feet and chest are often seen in the herding breeds.

create a trustworthy herding dog, shepherds selected and bred only those dogs that were aggressive enough to move the flocks, but that didn't attack them. A tendency to nip can still be seen in many of today's herding breeds.

One of the most popular herding dogs is the collie. This breed got its start in the hills of Scotland, where it was used to herd and guard sheep. There are two interesting stories as to how the collie got its name. *Col* is the Anglo-Saxon word for "black," and some people think that collies were named after the black-faced sheep they tended. *Collie* is also a Gaelic word meaning "useful." There is certainly no doubt that these dogs were useful to the shepherds who kept them. Because they were frequently left alone with the sheep, collies had to be exceptionally gentle and trustworthy. It is these qualities that have made them such popular family pets.

Like many other herding dogs, the collie has a long, thick coat to protect it from the cold. Its fur can be reddish-brown, tan, black, or a combination, with a white chest, four white feet, and a white tip on its tail. These white markings are a herding dog trademark. They are also found in several other herding dog breeds: the Border collie, the Shetland sheepdog, the Australian shepherd, and the Cardigan Welsh corgi. (The Pembroke Welsh corgi has four white feet but no white tail tip, because this breed has no tail at all!)

What's the reason for the white markings? In the northern parts of Britain, where many of the herding breeds were developed, the daylight hours are short for much of the year. Shepherds often have to work after dark, and it may be that they selected dogs with white markings because white is easier to see in dim light. If the white patches are on the dog's "moving parts"—the feet and tip of the tail—they are especially visible.

Though many herding dogs have white markings, there are none that are pure white. An all-white dog blends in so well that the sheep may overlook it. While this is fine for a sheep-guarding dog, a sheep-herding dog needs to be noticed. A dog with some black or other dark markings is much more likely to command the animals' attention.

A dog that looks like a miniature version of the collie, the Shetland sheepdog, originated in Scotland's Shetland Islands. These rugged, hilly islands are located as far north as Norway. Shetland Islanders must work hard to eke out a living in this harsh land. Fishing and raising sheep are their two main occupations. During the short summers, the sheep are driven up into the hills or ferried to outlying islands to graze. Sheepdogs were originally sent along to keep the flock together and to provide some protection against other animals. The Shetland sheepdog is not large enough to be much of a guard dog, but its loud bark effectively drives away wild animals and sounds an alarm. To this day, Shelties are known as a particularly noisy breed.

The black-and-white Border collie (which comes from an area along the border between England and Scotland) works with livestock in a unique way. Instead of barking and nipping, this dog controls the animals by staring at them. A Border collie at work crouches low to the ground and circles the flock, all the while fixing the sheep with a penetrating stare. Doing this, the collie seems remarkably like a hungry wolf "testing" its prey. Unlike a wolf, however, the Border collie never follows through with an attack. Because of their special skill in controlling livestock, Border collies are sometimes known as "eye dogs."

With its thick mop of hair, the Old English sheepdog could never be called an eye dog. Indeed, it's surprising that this dog can see at all. The Old English sheepdog is a more traditional

Because of its size and strength, the Old English sheepdog was used for guarding, as well as herding.

type of herding dog, moving the stock along by barking, nipping or just pushing the animals in the desired direction. Because of its size and strength, the Old English sheepdog originally worked as a combination herd and guard dog. It was also used to drive sheep and cattle to market.

Because they worked for a living, Old English sheepdogs were not subject to the medieval dog tax that was imposed on hunting breeds. The sign of a working shepherd's dog was a docked tail, so Old English sheepdogs (as well as some other herding breeds) usually had their tails bobbed at an early age. Though the original reason for it has passed, the custom of docking the tails of sheepdog puppies has continued to this day.

What can you expect if you choose one of the herding breeds as a pet? First of all, you'll be getting an active dog. Herding dogs are born to run, and a working collie or sheepdog may cover more than twenty miles in a single day. Don't get a herding dog if you cannot give it enough exercise.

Like other dogs that were expected to live outdoors, most herding breeds have long, thick fur. They shed quite a bit and need frequent brushing to look their best.

On the plus side, most herding dogs are fairly easy to train. Over the years, they have worked closely with people, who have expected them to be reliable and obedient helpers. Rounding up a flock of sheep, a dog might be several hundred yards away from the shepherd. A dog that did whatever it wanted would be no help at all. The shepherd needed a dog that would understand and obey commands, even at a great distance. As a result, herding breeds have been selected for their obedience and their quick learning abilities. The star among dogs when it comes to obedience is the German shepherd. This breed's intelligence and ability to learn have made it a natural for police-dog work. In fact, the

Originally a herding and guarding breed, the German shepherd now does many jobs. Above, a Seeing Eye dog. Below, a drug-sniffing dog helps Customs officers search for contraband.

German shepherd has been fighting crime for so long that many people have forgotten its original job: herding and protecting sheep.

Centuries of guarding livestock have made the herding breeds exceptionally good watchdogs. They were never bred or trained to attack and are much more likely to bark at an intruder than to go after him. Some breeds, like the Shetland sheepdog, are extremely alert and may bark at the slightest noise. This is a good thing to keep in mind if you live in an apartment with thin walls!

Even if they have never seen a sheep or cow, many herding dogs show typical herding behaviors. For example, they may try to round up groups of children or animals and push them into a corner. Though they rarely bite hard, these dogs may also nip at people when they are excited. These behaviors are natural ones for herding dogs, but they can be frightening to people who don't understand them.

Finally, herding dogs have a very sensitive chase response. This, combined with their need for exercise, sometimes causes them to chase cars and other animals. Fortunately, this problem can be easily solved: keep your pet in a fenced yard or on a leash.

10

To the Hunt: The Hounds

Dogs that pulled sleds, guarded property, and tended livestock have been a great help to people over the years. Without these canine assistants, life would have been much harder. And without dogs to help them hunt, people might never have survived at all. Hunters used dogs to help them capture the elusive animals of the forest and the swift animals of the plains. Even after they found other ways of getting food, people continued to hunt for sport and continued to use dogs to help them. The dogs they used were hounds. Different hounds hunted in different ways. Some followed their noses, tracking their prey by smell. Others relied on their keen vision to spot the prey and on their long, powerful legs to run it down.

Because of their excellent vision, these latter dogs were called sight hounds, or gaze hounds. They are among the most ancient of all dogs. In fact, one of the sight hounds, the saluki, is thought to be the world's oldest purebred dog. Sight hounds have changed very little over thousands of years. Middle Eastern carvings from the year 6000 B.C. show animals being chased by dogs that look remarkably like today's salukis.

Gazelles, antelopes, and other speedy animals were the prey of the first sight hounds. On the flat, open plains of Egypt and the Middle East, nomadic tribes hunted with salukis and greyhounds. Sometimes these dogs were used in combination with trained falcons. When the hunters spotted their quarry, the falcons were released to fly around the head of the prey animal until the dogs could overtake it and bring it down.

The sight hounds were, and still are, silent hunters. Unlike the scent hounds that we'll meet later, the sight hounds never bark while pursuing their prey. One reason for this may be that it is hard to run thirty miles an hour and bark at the same time! Another is that, on the open plains, the hunters could easily see the direction the hounds had taken. There was no need for the dogs to signal their location by barking.

Different parts of the world had their own versions of the sight hound. Another gazelle hunter, the Afghan hound, is a native of Afghanistan. This breed has a longer coat than its southern relatives to keep it warm in Afghanistan's cold winters.

By the fourth century B.C., sight hounds were known in Europe. Scottish deerhounds and Irish wolfhounds were used as hunters in their native countries. The Irish wolfhound was so good at its job that, by the 1700s, there were no wolves left at all in Britain. This enormous dog is the largest and sturdiest of the sight hounds. In all likelihood, one of its ancestors was another huge dog, the Great Dane.

Russia had its own wolf hunter, the borzoi, or Russian wolfhound. Legend has it that a seventeenth-century Russian nobleman imported greyhoundlike dogs from the Middle East to use for hunting. When the dogs arrived, he discovered that they could not tolerate Russia's cold climate, so they were mated with a thick-coated collielike dog. The dog that eventually resulted was the borzoi. Borzois usually hunted in pairs or small groups. When pursuing a wolf, two or three dogs would race up alongside the animal. The dogs would lock their jaws onto the wolf's neck, wrestle it to the ground, and hold it there until the hunter arrived.

These days we think of sight hounds as aristocratic, elegant dogs. In the seventeenth and eighteenth centuries, too, they were the dogs of royalty. Hunting was an upper class sport and only the wealthiest noblemen were allowed to stalk game in the royal forests. It was against the law for common people to hunt in these forests. In fact, they were not even permitted to own sight-hunting dogs.

When the sport of dog racing became popular, sight hounds finally fell into the hands of the common people. The newest sight hound, the whippet, was developed just over a hundred years ago by coal miners in England. By breeding a greyhoundlike dog with a terrier, they produced a small, lightning fast dog that was known as the "poor man's race horse." Whippets and greyhounds are still used today for dog racing.

Just by looking at a sight hound—whether it is a greyhound, a borzoi, or an Afghan hound—you can tell that it was born to run. Its legs are long and strong, its body is lean, and its chest is deep to hold the large heart and lungs needed for constant running.

A dog keeps cool by panting through its mouth and nose. The sight hound's long, pointed nose serves as an efficient cooling system for this active dog.

Because vision is all-important to the sight hound, its eyes are large and are never covered by hair. Hearing is less important, as you can tell from the drooping ears.

The most obvious thing to consider if you want a sight hound for a pet is whether you'll be able to give it enough exercise.

Though most of these dogs are not very active indoors, once they get outside they want to run. A slow walk around the block is just not enough! Because of their history, they are also likely to chase cats, cars, bicycles, and any other moving object. Whatever they chase, they will probably try to bite.

It's good to keep in mind that sight hounds were created to work, not to be pets. The hunters who bred these dogs did not care what their personalities were like—what mattered was that they ran fast, hunted well, and did not fight too much with other dogs. Owners of sight hounds sometimes say that their dogs are aloof and not very sociable around people. A sight hound's best friend (if it has one) is likely to be another dog, rather than a person.

Some sight hounds, especially the frail, thin breeds, can be nervous and high-strung. These dogs need quiet surroundings, so a noisy city apartment is not for them.

Because barking was never a big part of their job, most sight hounds are quiet dogs. An advantage of having a quiet pet is that your neighbors will never complain about the noise. A disadvantage is that your dog will be less inclined to bark when someone comes to the door. Sight hounds have rarely been used as guards, so they are not as protective of their territory as other breeds. Some, like the slender greyhound and whippet, are just not brawny enough to be very effective guard dogs. Others, like the Irish wolfhound and Scottish deerhound, will frighten intruders simply because of their enormous size.

The Irish wolfhound, perhaps because of its Great Dane ancestry, is a rugged dog. It is also friendlier and more playful than most other sight hounds. Of all the sight hounds, this breed probably makes one of the best family pets. It likes to play and can stand more roughhousing than a fragile greyhound or whippet.

Though they are both classified as hounds, sight hounds and scent hounds differ tremendously. While sight hounds are tall and elegant, most scent hounds are shorter. Scent hounds specialize in following their noses and, as every dog knows, the best smells are down near the earth.

Scent hounds are also noisier than their sight hound cousins. Because they often tracked their prey through dense forests, it was necessary for these dogs to telegraph their location to their human partners. They did this by barking loudly and continuously. When a fox or raccoon was cornered, the baying of the hounds quickly let the hunter know where his quarry—and his dogs—could be found.

The most famous scent hound is, of course, the bloodhound. The ancestors of this breed were known as early as the third century A.D. for their amazing sense of smell. The bloodhound is better than any other breed at following a scent trail, even if the trail is several days old. Some people believe that the bloodhound's drooping ears and the heavy folds of skin on its face help to trap scent molecules so the ultrasensitive nose can detect them.

During the Middle Ages bloodhounds were used to hunt stags and, later on, to track down criminals and missing persons. In the United States there are stories of fierce bloodhounds pursuing runaway slaves in the South. Dogs may have been used for this grim task, but they were probably not bloodhounds. These dogs are, in reality, very gentle animals. Their speciality is finding their prey, not attacking it.

As time went on, many forests were cleared and large animals like the stag became harder to find. People began to hunt foxes and hares instead. Fox hunting has remained popular in England to this day. Foxes were swifter animals than stags, and hunters found that their heavy hounds were too slow. To produce a faster

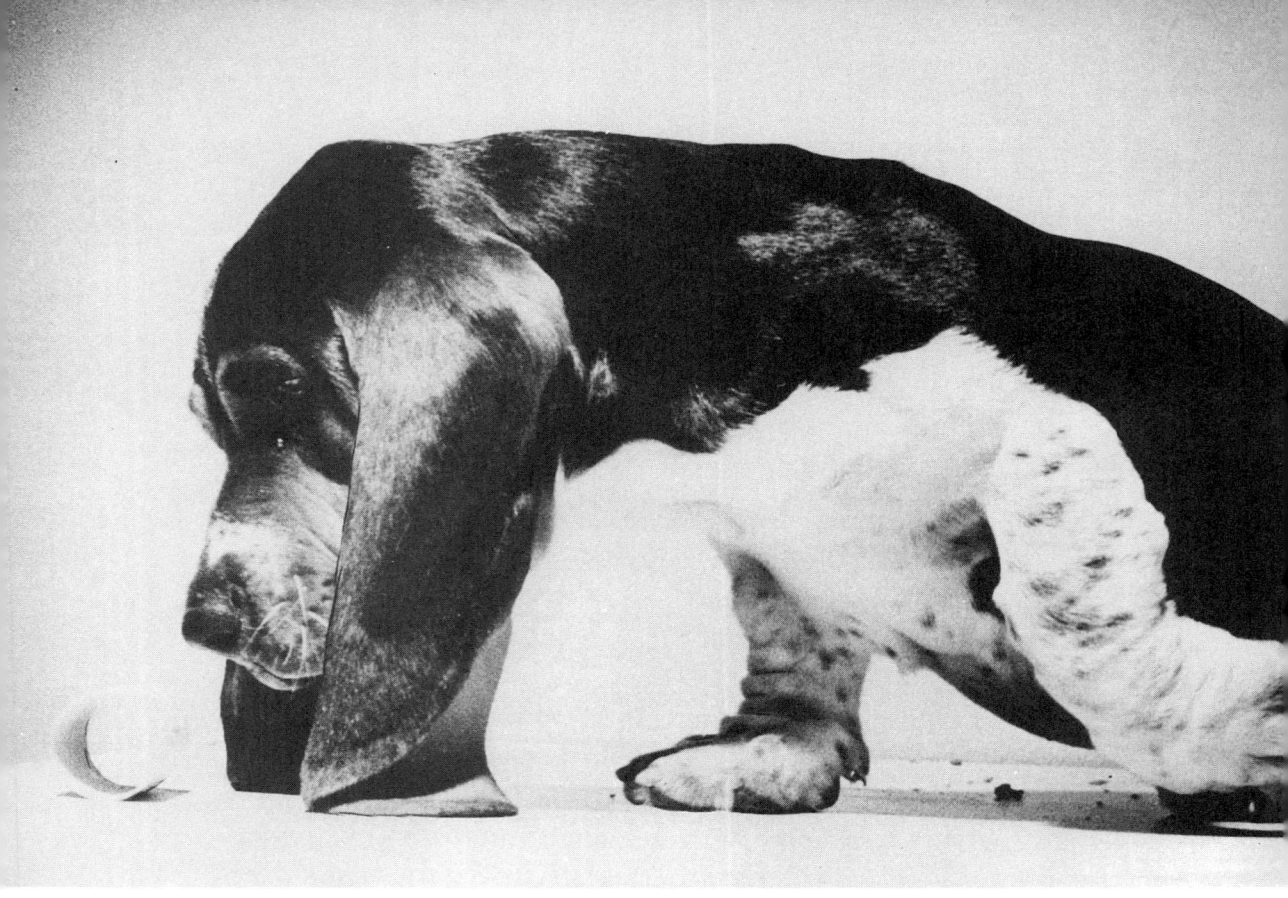

The basset hound's compact body and keen sense of smell made it perfectly suited for tracking small prey through the underbrush.

dog, a bloodhoundlike dog known as the Talbot hound was crossed with a greyhound. The dog that resulted, the foxhound, was so fast that hunters had to follow on horseback and communicate with their dogs by means of hunting horns. The beagle, which looks like a smaller version of the foxhound, was also used for this type of hunting.

Smaller game, such as rabbits and badgers, could be hunted on foot. The ideal dog was one that was fast enough to keep up with the prey, but not so fast that the hunter would lose it in the underbrush. The basset hound, from France, and the dachshund, from Germany, were developed for just this purpose. With their short legs, there was a limit to how fast they could run. And because they were close to the ground, it was easy for them to follow the scent of their prey.

The dachshund, whose name means badger dog, was somewhat unusual for a hound. Not only did this brave little dog track down badgers, he pursued them into their underground dens! As we'll see later, this kind of behavior is more typical of terriers than of hounds.

More than most other dogs, scent hounds are accustomed to working in groups. Even when they were not out hunting, packs of hounds were kept together in kennels rather than indoors as house pets. In the kennels it was important to have dogs that got along well and did not fight. As a result, most scent hounds have been selected for their sociable, outgoing dispositions. They are friendly with just about everyone, and fit in particularly well with

Also a hunter, the little dachshund fearlessly followed badgers into their underground burrows.

large families. If you have other dogs, a scent hound will probably adjust contentedly to its new pack. In fact, it will be happier if it is *not* your only dog. However, cats, rabbits, and other small pets that resemble the scent hound's prey are likely to be chased.

Because they were never expected to work closely with people, scent hounds may be a bit harder to train than some other breeds. In this respect they are quite a bit like the polar dogs: friendly and outgoing, but not very obedient.

Part of a scent hound's job is barking and howling to let the hunter know where the pack is. A strong "voice" is considered essential for a working hound, and hunters have even bred dogs for the sound of their bark. No matter what the occasion, a scent hound is likely to respond by making noise. This can sometimes cause problems, especially when the dog is left alone. Because they are so sociable, scent hounds dislike being by themselves even more than other dogs do. All dogs have a tendency to howl when separated from the pack but, in the scent hound, this behavior is practically guaranteed.

One positive thing about their tendency to make noise is that it makes scent hounds very good watchdogs. Scent hounds have never been used as guards and are actually not very protective, but their constant barking makes them seem as though they are.

Finally, if you get one of these breeds, make sure your yard is securely fenced and always walk your pet on a leash. The instinct to follow an interesting smell is so strong that it overcomes almost everything else. A scent hound with its nose to the ground may wander miles away from home, never to be seen again.

11

Bird Dogs Extraordinaire: The Sporting Breeds

Following the scent of game is a skill hounds share with another canine group: sporting dogs. Both hounds and sporting dogs are hunters, but they work in very different ways.

While hounds track game with their noses to the ground, many sporting dogs (particularly the pointers and setters) work with their heads up, scenting the air. As we saw, wolves use both of these techniques to locate their prey. Hounds and sporting dogs have simply specialized in different aspects of the wolf's behavior.

When hounds get the scent of an animal, they take off after it, barking excitedly. A pack of hounds will continue to pursue the prey until it has been cornered underground or chased up a tree. If the hounds can get to it, they may try to kill the prey themselves.

Sporting dogs, on the other hand, never follow through with the chase and attack. Their job is not to do the hunting, but rather to assist the human hunter by finding, flushing out, or retrieving the game. These dogs work quietly so as not to scare away birds, and, like all good assistants, they obey their master's commands to the letter.

Sporting dogs are sometimes referred to as gun dogs. This name is a bit misleading, as most of these dogs were helping hunters long before guns were invented. During the Middle Ages, when hunters used nets and trained hawks or falcons to trap their prey, little dogs known as spaniels were popular hunting assistants. These dogs were common in Spain, and many people believe that they got their name from the Latin word for that country: Hispania.

Once they had located the game, spaniels either "set" or "flushed" it. The job of a setting spaniel was to drop to the ground and lie motionless when it discovered a hidden bird. The hunters then crept up and threw out a large net, trapping both bird and dog. The setting spaniels later developed into the setters we know today: the English setter, the Irish setter, and the Gordon setter.

In other cases, spaniels were trained to find birds and drive them out of the underbrush so that they could be pursued by falcons. These dogs were called "springing spaniels" because of their talent for springing or flushing birds from their hiding places. Modern-day springer spaniels and cocker spaniels (so named for their speciality in tracking woodcock) are descendants of these early springing spaniels.

Spaniels frequently had to track their prey through dense shrubs and tangled thickets. Their small bodies and short, powerful legs allowed them to move through areas that would be off-limits to larger dogs, and their long, silken hair protected them from the underbrush. Their tails were often docked to prevent them from being caught in the brambles. The high, rounded forehead, a characteristic of all modern spaniels, probably helped to shield their eyes against branches.

After guns were invented, the spaniel's color became an important consideration. Snuffling through the bushes, a dog could easily blend in with the landscape and be shot accidentally. For

All sporting dogs, whether setters (above) or spaniels (below), have been bred to work closely with their human partners. This characteristic has made them popular pets.

this reason, many working spaniels, such as the clumber, the Brittany, the springer, and the cocker, had distinctive white markings. These markings can still be seen in the first three breeds and in some modern cocker spaniels.

The spaniels were fine for hunting in thick cover, but for hunting on open fields, a larger, faster dog was needed. This dog was the pointer. Though it became popular only during the last few hundred years, the pointer is actually one of the most ancient hunting dogs. A limestone tablet dating from the year 2000 B.C. shows the Egyptian pharaoh Antefaa II surrounded by four dogs, one of which was a pointer! This dog's talent lay in following its nose to where game was hidden and then freezing with one foot raised and head pointed in the direction of the concealed animal. Pointing is a behavior that can sometimes be seen in wolves. When a wolf hunting in a pack discovers a hidden animal, it often freezes until other pack members arrive and flush out the prey.

All the pointing breeds—the pointer, the weimaraner, the vizsla, and others—are leaner and faster than other sporting dogs. It is likely that early pointers were crossed with greyhounds to improve their speed. This would help explain their streamlined bodies and their need for lots of activity.

The fourth member of the sporting group, the retriever, has a much shorter history than spaniels, setters, or pointers. Retrievers did not become popular until the nineteenth century, when people began to use guns for hunting. Although guns had been around for several hundred years already, the early models were inaccurate and sometimes dangerous. As time went on, gun design improved. By the nineteenth century, hunters were using guns rather than nets and falcons to bag their prey. Now that they could shoot birds from far away, hunters needed dogs that could spot where the birds had fallen and retrieve them. This required

Bird Dogs Extraordinaire: *The Sporting Breeds*

not only a keen sense of smell, but superior eyesight as well.

In the early 1800s there already existed a dog with these qualities that specialized in retrieving. This was the Saint John's dog, an early version of today's Labrador retriever. Though these dogs were retrievers, they were not yet used by hunters. Instead, they worked with the fishermen who netted cod off the banks of Newfoundland. The job of the Saint John's dogs was to dive into the water after fish, nets, or buoys that had washed overboard. Eventually, travelers brought the dogs to England, where sportsmen quickly recognized their value as hunting companions.

Labrador retrievers are as much at home in the water as they are on dry land.

Like pointing, retrieving is a behavior that can be seen in wild wolves on a hunt. After they have made a kill, wolves will often bring food back to the den for the pups and pregnant females. Over the years, dog breeders have selected and strengthened this "bringing back" behavior to create our modern-day retrievers.

The job of a hunting retriever is somewhat different from that of a spaniel, setter, or pointer. While these dogs are actively involved in the hunt, finding game and flushing it out of the bushes, retrievers go to work only after the shooting stops. During the hunt a retriever is expected to sit quietly next to its master, waiting for the signal to go after a fallen bird. While waiting, the dog is alert and watchful, scanning the sky for birds and marking where they fall. To do this job successfully, the retriever must be a fast learner and have an excellent memory. There are stories of hunting retrievers able to memorize the locations of six or more birds!

Because they are intelligent, patient, and easy to train, retrievers make ideal guide dogs. Both Labrador and golden retrievers are widely used for this important work.

Most retrievers love the water, and some have been especially bred to be water dogs. These include the Chesapeake Bay retriever, the curly coated retriever, the Irish water spaniel, and—surprise!—the poodle. All these breeds have curly or wavy coats with a layer of oil to repel water.

The poodle has been bred as a pet for so long that many people have forgotten its history as a water retriever. In fact, the American Kennel Club does not list the poodle as a retriever, but instead places it in the nonsporting group, along with such breeds as the Boston terrier and the bulldog.

Although many people think of them as French, poodles actually originated in Germany. The name poodle comes from the German word *puddeln*, which means "to paddle or splash." The

The poodle's curly coat is one clue to this breed's origin as a water retriever. Most poodles now "work" as pets.

fancy hairstyles of today's poodles were originally done for convenience. If left unclipped, a working poodle's thick coat would quickly become matted and caked with mud.

One of the most popular styles was the continental clip (sometimes also called the lion clip). The hair on the dog's hindquarters and legs was cut very short, to allow the animal to swim more easily, while the hair on the shoulders and chest was left long (like a lion's mane), to protect it from the cold. Even the little poufs of hair on the legs and at the tip of the tail had a purpose.

The "bracelets" kept the dog's ankles warm and the hair on the tail served as a flag, making the dog easy to spot.

One of a working retriever's most important jobs is to bring back game in good condition. To accomplish this, the retriever uses its mouth very gently, never biting down on the object it is carrying. In fact, retrievers are not very likely to bite at all, especially when compared to the nippy herding dogs or aggressive terriers. The "soft mouth" is one characteristic that makes retrievers such reliable family pets. They will bring back your newspaper in good shape and they won't bite the mail carrier, either.

It is not only the retrievers that are good as pets. The cocker spaniel and the Irish setter both rank in the top-ten list of popular dog breeds. The main reason that sporting dogs are such great companions is that they were bred to work very closely with their human partners. Obedience was essential. After all, no one wanted a hunting dog that would frighten the birds or, worse yet, try to bite them. In general, sporting dogs are easy to train, very obedient, and not likely to attack other animals or people.

Since a barking dog would scare the birds away, the sporting breeds are usually fairly quiet. They are also calm and not easily upset—a necessity for a dog that worked in the midst of booming gunfire all day. While many dogs are terrified of thunder, a sporting dog will probably sleep right through even the loudest storms.

Sporting dogs are people-oriented and they need plenty of human contact. If left alone for too long, they become quite anxious. We saw earlier what can happen when an anxious dog has the house to itself. If you get a sporting dog, plan on spending plenty of time with it.

Like all dogs bred to work outdoors, these breeds need exercise. The ones with the biggest exercise requirements are those that cover the most ground: the long-legged pointers and setters.

Because strict obedience is so important for a hunting dog, the sporting breeds have been bred and trained to think of humans as the alpha members of the pack. To show that they know their place, these dogs perform many submissive behaviors—licking, tail wagging, and so on. This is why we think of them as being so friendly. Unfortunately, being submissive has its drawbacks. The sporting breeds are not likely to dominate their owners, but they won't dominate anybody else, either. For this reason, they are not the world's best guard dogs.

Finally, keep in mind that the sporting breeds started out as bird dogs, and many of them are still very interested in anything that flies. If your hobby is raising canaries, you may want to think twice before getting one of these dogs. In a house full of birds, your pet may spend its time pointing, flushing, or trying to retrieve, depending on its specialty.

12

Feisty Fighters: The Terriers

*I*f hounds and sporting dogs were the companions of the rich, then terriers were the dogs of the common people. Terriers were, for the most part, scruffy little animals, a far cry from their elegant cousins the spaniels and retrievers. Looks were not so important to the working-class people who kept terriers. What mattered was that the dogs did their job. Like sporting dogs, terriers were hunters. But this was hunting of quite a different sort. Sporting dogs were bred and trained to assist their masters, either by finding game, flushing it out of the bushes, or retrieving it once it had been shot. The one thing these dogs never did was to kill the prey themselves.

Terriers, on the other hand, were expected to do it all. People kept terriers to control "pests"—the foxes that threatened their livestock, the rats that infested their homes, and so on. Though small, these pests could be vicious, and catching them was not easy. When pursued, they fled into underground burrows and lashed out savagely at any animal that tried to enter. The terrier's job was to capture them, even if that meant tunneling into a fox den and dragging the prey to the surface.

To do this, a terrier had to be small enough to fit into an underground burrow and brave enough to face the angry fox or badger within. A good hunting terrier would take on animals much larger than itself and would keep on fighting, even when hurt. This never-say-die attitude earned the terrier a reputation as an especially courageous—and stubborn—dog. As we'll see later, these qualities can still be seen in the terriers of today.

Terriers have been going about their pest-killing business for a very long time. Roman troops invading Britain two thousand years ago brought back tales of the little dogs that pursued their prey below ground. It was the Romans who gave these dogs their name, *terrarii,* from the Latin word for earth. Later on they were also called "earth dogges" and were known for their spunky personalities as well as for their skill as hunters.

Up until the 1800s there were only two kinds of terrier. One was a little dog with short, powerful legs, used for digging small prey out of their underground dens. These dogs had compact bodies, which allowed them to burrow into the tiniest spaces, and dense, wiry coats that offered protection against the elements. They were the ancestors of such small breeds as the cairn terrier, the Scottish terrier, and the Skye terrier.

The other kind of terrier was bigger and had longer legs. Some think that these dogs were crossbred with greyhounds to improve their speed. They were, indeed, fast runners and were sometimes used along with packs of hounds to hunt foxes and otters. The terriers joined in the chase and, once the hounds had cornered the prey, the terriers went in to do the dirty work. Modern breeds descended from this large dog include the Airedale and the fox terrier.

During the nineteenth century people began to breed terriers to do different, specialized jobs, and soon distinct breeds emerged.

With gentle, consistent obedience training, even the most stubborn terrier makes a great companion.

Today the American Kennel Club lists twenty-four different terrier breeds.

Most terriers originated in the British Isles, as you can tell from their names: Manchester terrier, Norfolk terrier, and Staffordshire bull terrier, to name a few. The Scottish terrier came from the western highlands of Scotland and the Skye terrier from the Isle of Skye, just off Scotland's coast. Another Scotsman is the cairn terrier, a compact, rough-coated dog. The cairn terrier got its name in an interesting way. Centuries ago, the Scottish people honored their dead by piling up rocks into huge mounds, called cairns. These cairns provided good hiding places for small game. Hunters needed a little dog that could wriggle in between the rocks and drive out the prey. The dog they chose, the cairn terrier, was named after the rock piles in which it hunted.

Another breed with a fascinating history is the West Highland white terrier. It is thought that this dog was bred from the cairn terrier in the late 1800s. Then, as now, people had certain expectations about the color of their dogs. Cairn terriers were allowed to be black, red, silver—in fact, any color except white. If a litter occasionally included a white puppy, the owners made sure not to breed it.

One day, however, a Scottish colonel and dog lover named E. D. Malcolm discovered that a white dog had certain advantages. Out hunting with a pack of cairns, Colonel Malcolm mistook one of his dogs for a rabbit and accidentally shot it. Heartbroken, he realized he needed a dog that could be seen more easily in the dark heather. From then on, he bred only the rare white cairn terriers, and eventually a new breed was established: the West Highland white terrier, or Westie for short.

Ireland, Wales, and England had their share of terriers as well. From Ireland came the Irish and Kerry blue terriers and from Wales the Welsh and Sealyham terriers. Nine different terriers came from England alone. Frequently the breeds were named after the place where they originated. The Airedale, for example, got its start in England's Yorkshire district, in a town beside the River Aire. These large dogs were used to hunt otters, weasels, foxes, and water rats.

The Manchester terrier, from northwest England, was a champion rat catcher. In the 1800s killing rats was a sport, as well as a necessity. Owners of Manchester terriers often entered their dogs in rat-killing competitions. A legendary Manchester terrier named Billy is said to have finished off one hundred rats in just six minutes!

Throughout history, dogs have been used in cruel "sports" such as this. Contests in which dogs were pitted against bears or bulls were popular, and the dog most often used in these spectacles was the bulldog. The bulldog was very powerful, but not very quick. After a time, the bulldog was crossed with the Old English terrier, a breed that is now extinct. The result was a stocky, muscular dog with the strength of a bulldog and the speed of a terrier. The bull and terrier, as it was first called, was the ancestor of several modern breeds: the bull terrier; the Staffordshire bull terrier; and its New-World counterpart, the American Staffordshire terrier.

Like its descendants, the bull and terrier could be a fearsome fighter. After bull baiting was outlawed in 1835, it was used in another popular, though illegal, pastime: dogfighting. In this competition, two dogs were placed in a pit (hence the name pit bull terrier) and allowed to fight until one was killed or injured too badly to continue. To be a successful fighter, a dog could not give up, even if it were hurt.

If we look at terriers in light of wolf behavior, we'll see that they act a lot like alpha wolves. Being dominant comes naturally to them; giving in to another animal (or human being) does not. Though it's more obvious in fighting dogs, a stubborn streak can be seen in almost all terriers. As hunters, they had to be brave (or crazy) enough to face a fierce enemy and keep on battling even when things got tough. Terriers were not bred to hold back their attack, as herding and sporting dogs were. Because of this, they are much more likely to bite, especially when they feel threatened. They may also attack without warning—after all, a surprise attack was probably the best way to catch a rat or badger. To top it off, their teeth and jaws are uncommonly strong for such a small dog.

All this means that terriers can be difficult to train. They consider themselves top dog, and don't much like being told what to

This terrier's willingness to take on any opponent has made the pit bull a favorite of dogfighters.

do. And heaven help the terrier owner who disciplines his or her pet with a rolled-up newspaper! Threatening this type of dog will just make it angry. (Actually, you should never train any dog by hitting it when it misbehaves. A better method is to reward the dog for the things it does right.)

On the plus side, the aggressive little terrier makes a terrific watchdog. As their pricked ears suggest, terriers have excellent hearing. Years of hunting have made them alert to the slightest sound. Like alpha wolves, they patrol their territory with special care and bark to warn the pack of any disturbance. Their protective nature helps explain why terriers seem to bark more than many other dogs.

Like any dog that was bred to run and hunt outdoors, terriers need a lot of exercise. Whether this is good or bad depends on you. If you are very active, an energetic terrier may be the perfect pet. But if you'd rather stay inside reading or watching television, a slower and more relaxed dog might be a better choice.

By all means, don't get a terrier if you cannot give it enough exercise. To burn off that extra energy, a frustrated terrier may bark, run around, and get into trouble. Terriers specialize in digging, perhaps because of their history as underground hunters. It is not uncommon for a terrier cooped up in a small yard to tunnel under the fence to freedom.

Finally, consider the other animals in your home before you get a terrier. Many terriers will fit right in with a house full of pets. But some, especially those with fighting pedigrees, may expect to be top dog. If there is already a dominant dog in the household, you can expect problems. Some (but certainly not all) terriers may have trouble adjusting to cats, rabbits, and other small pets because of their resemblance to the animals they once hunted. Living with a terrier may be a bit more challenging than living with another type of dog, but if you want a pet that is lively, fun-loving, and full of energy, a terrier makes a great companion.

13

Just Friends: The Companion Breeds

All the dogs we've met were originally created to do some type of work—herding, guarding, hunting, and so on. For most of them, those jobs are a thing of the past and they "work" now at being pets. One group of dogs, however, was designed from the very beginning to lead a pampered life, doing no job other than keeping people company. Some of these dogs, like the Maltese and the Pekingese, were distinct breeds, while others, like the Italian greyhound and the toy poodle, were miniature versions of larger dogs.

Because these dogs did not work, there was no need for them to have any special skills. They didn't have to be strong enough to pull a sled or brave enough to go after a badger or sharp-eyed enough to spot and retrieve a bird. What they did have to be was small—small enough to live inside the house, to sit on a lady's lap, or to be carried around in an emperor's sleeve. Most of these breeds are still very tiny, weighing in at ten pounds or less—about the size of a house cat.

These days, lots of people have dogs as pets. But in the past, only the wealthy could afford to keep a dog that didn't work for

One of the earliest companion breeds, the Pekingese enjoyed a pampered life with Chinese royalty.

a living. It is not surprising, then, that many of the companion breeds started out as pets of the rich and powerful.

We've already met one royal bred: the Pekingese. The Maltese is another. This breed's ancestors were most likely northern dogs that traveled south along the trade routes to the Mediterranean. Some ended up on the island of Malta. Though it was a small island, Malta was an important center of commerce. When goods were shipped to the Middle East and the Orient, the exotic, white dogs of Malta were sometimes part of the cargo. In this way the Maltese made its way to other parts of the world.

In Tibet the Maltese helped to found two other breeds, the Tibetan terrier and the Lhasa apso. Some people think that the breed is an ancestor of the Pekingese as well. Maltese blood can even be seen in the bichon frise, which for years was found mainly in the Canary Islands. This breed was originally called *bichon à poil frisé,* which means "lap dog with curly hair." The bichon does, indeed, resemble a Maltese with a permanent.

Throughout history Maltese dogs have been the pets of royalty. The Roman emperor Claudius had a Maltese. Publius, an early Roman governor of Malta, owned a tiny Maltese named Issa. Publius loved his dog so much that he commissioned an artist to paint its portrait.

It is said that Marie Antoinette, queen of France, was greatly attached to a Maltese named Thisbee. There are reports that the little dog leaped to its death from a bridge over the river Seine on October 16, 1793, the same day that Marie Antoinette went to the guillotine. (It's hard to tell whether this fantastic story is true. Other sources say that the queen's companion during her last days was a Pomeranian!)

One of the best known toy breeds, the Chihuahua, had its origins on the other side of the world. The ancestors of the modern-day Chihuahua played an important role in the culture of Mexico's Aztec Indians. It was Aztec custom, when someone died, to sacrifice a small dog and bury it along with the body. The Aztecs believed that the dog, with its mystical powers, would guide the dead person's soul safely across the nine deadly rivers of the underworld. Dogs that escaped being sacrificed often met an equally unpleasant end. The Aztecs considered dogs a delicacy, and frequently fattened and ate them! Today's Chihuahuas are luckier than their ancestors—their only job is being pets.

Of all the modern breeds, the miniature dogs seem the most different from their wolf ancestors. Unlike wolves, they could never survive on their own. These little dogs are totally dependent upon people for their survival. They do need to be protected, but some people go too far, pampering their tiny pets as if they were babies.

When a dog is spoiled and allowed to have its own way all the time, it begins to get the idea that it is the leader of the pack. The result is a dog that stubbornly refuses to obey the commands of its lower-ranking packmates. It will not come when called, walk on a leash, or even eat its dinner if it doesn't feel like it. This is just as likely to happen with small dogs as it is with big ones. Actually, it is even more likely to happen with small dogs because people have a greater tendency to spoil these tiny "helpless" pets. The result, ridiculous as it seems, can be a miniscule dog that literally rules the roost: barking aggressively, biting people, and terrorizing anyone who enters the house. Though an aggressive Chihuahua is not as big a threat as an aggressive Great Dane, these behaviors can still be annoying and dangerous.

Obedience training is just as important for the miniature breeds as it is for larger dogs, and it is the only way to let your pet know who's boss. Unfortunately, some pet owners do not think it is necessary, because these dogs are so small and seem so easy to control. After all, if your Shih Tzu refuses to walk by your side, you can always pick it up and carry it—something that would never be possible with a Saint Bernard! Because so many owners put up with misbehavior and don't bother to train their little dogs, some of these breeds have earned a reputation as being stubborn, demanding, and difficult to control. This doesn't have to be the case. Most of these dogs are quite intelligent and responsive to training if you take the time to work with them.

For some people who own toy dogs, their pets are more than just companions—they are status symbols. The Yorkshire terrier, with its long, silky fur, and the toy poodle, with its elaborate hairdo, show the world that their masters have money to spend on luxuries. Because they have been bred for their exotic ap-

The toy breeds may be tiny, but they need obedience training as much as their larger relatives do.

pearance, they require frequent grooming to look their best. The Yorkie, for instance, must be brushed almost daily to keep its long coat free of tangles, and the toy poodle needs regular (and expensive) haircuts. If you get one of these breeds, you should plan on spending a lot of time with a brush in your hand or a lot of money at the groomer.

Since they are so small, the miniature breeds make good pets for people who live in apartments. Like all dogs, they need to run, but they can usually get most of the exercise they need by racing around inside the house. When you do take them outdoors, it is a good idea to bundle them up in a sweater or jacket. Small dogs, dogs with thin coats, and dogs with slender builds tend to be quite sensitive to the cold.

Small dogs do not take up as much space as large ones, and they don't eat as much, either. The money you save on food can be spent on grooming.

Despite their small size, these breeds are usually excellent watchdogs. They tend to bark quite a bit, and can set up a real racket when someone approaches the door. Luckily, the noise is enough to frighten most intruders. These dogs are simply too small to follow through on their threats.

The miniature breeds, like all the other dogs we've met in this section, can make wonderful companions as long as they are matched up with the right people. The first step in choosing the perfect dog is to decide what you want: a small, easy-to-care-for apartment pet, a rugged dog that likes to run and play outdoors, or a quiet dog that will sleep by the fire while guarding your home.

Personality is important, too. Do you want a dog that is outgoing and friendly or one that is a bit more aloof? A dog that will get along with other animals or one that prefers to be "top dog"? After you have decided what you're looking for, the descriptions in this chapter will give you an idea of the best type of dog for you. Then, before you make a final decision, go to the library and read more about the breed you're considering. Knowing all you can about your new pet is the best way to make sure you'll be happy together.

PART FOUR

Pit Bulls and Pekingese: What We've Done to Dogs

14

Dog Problems

*I*magine what would happen if a Siberian husky and a Pekingese were stranded in a forest and left to fend for themselves. Which breed do you think would be more likely to survive?

Both would have to struggle, but the husky would probably fare a lot better. Its dense fur would protect it from the nighttime chill, and its strong legs and sharp teeth would enable it to chase and kill small animals for food.

The Pekingese, on the other hand, would have a terrible time. Its silky, elegant fur would quickly become matted and tangled. It would not be able to run fast enough on its short legs to capture its dinner or even to escape a larger animal. And with its tiny teeth, it would have trouble eating anything but the softest food.

Over the years, people have used selective breeding to create many different dogs for many different purposes. Some, like the husky, are still very similar to their wolf ancestors. Others, like the Pekingese, are about as different from wolves as one could imagine. In general, the more "unwolflike" dogs become, the harder it is for them to survive on their own. Sometimes, they even have difficulty living in the protected world they share with humans. In these cases, people have taken selective breeding too far, and the dogs have paid the price.

The toy breeds have had an especially difficult time. In their desire for small house pets, people have bred these dogs to be so tiny that some, like the teacup poodle, are barely bigger than a kitten. For a dog this small, even a walk outdoors is a dangerous undertaking. Other dogs and people loom over them like giants, and simple things such as stairs, curbs, and subway gratings are major obstacles. Considering the hazards, it is no wonder these dogs are often carried everywhere by their owners.

Some toy dogs, especially Chihuahuas and toy poodles, seem to tremble all the time. It's not just because they are nervous—they are usually cold as well. Dogs this small have a very hard time keeping warm.

Other small breeds, such as the Pekingese, the pug, and the English toy spaniel, have been bred to look helpless and appealing, almost like human babies. With their round heads, large eyes, and little button noses, these dogs are undeniably cute. But in this case, being cute isn't much fun.

Most dogs with short noses also have small nostrils and cramped air passages. As a result, they sometimes have breathing difficulties, and they have trouble keeping cool when the temperature rises. Unlike people, dogs do not perspire. Instead, they cool off by panting through their nose and mouth. The longer a dog's nose, the better job it does keeping its canine owner cool. Unfortunately for flat-faced dogs, their small noses make very inefficient cooling systems. Because of this, they suffer greatly in the summer heat. If you have one of these breeds, it is good to keep in mind that it may have a hard time breathing, particularly in hot weather. Be especially careful not to leave your pet (or any animal) in the car when it's warm out, and make sure it has an air-conditioned place to rest during the summer.

Dogs with pushed-in faces also have smaller-than-normal jaws, so their teeth are crowded together. These dogs cannot gnaw bones or chew meat as well as wolves or other dogs can. If your dog seems to have trouble eating, ask your veterinarian for advice.

Another thing that sets these dogs apart from their wolf ancestors is their eyes. Instead of the wolf's narrow, slitlike eyes, these breeds have eyes that are large, round, and somewhat bulging. People probably selected for wide-open eyes because it made their dogs appear friendlier and less threatening. But prominent eyes

Our desire for dogs with a unique appearance has resulted in breeds that suffer from skin and eye trouble, crowded teeth, and a host of other problems.

can be a health hazard. If the dog does not blink enough, its eyes may dry out and become infected. What's more, the eyes are not well protected by the skull, so they are much more easily injured.

By now it probably seems that little dogs have all the problems. But very large breeds, too, have their share of difficulties. For one thing, they don't live as long. The average lifespan of a Great Dane, for instance, is about eight to ten years, compared to fifteen years or longer for most of the smaller breeds.

Large dogs are also prone to a condition known as hip dysplasia, in which the hip joints are badly formed. Hip dysplasia can cause even a very young dog to limp and have trouble walking. As the dog grows older, the problem gets worse.

Dachshunds and Welsh corgis may also have problems as they age but, in these breeds, the weak spot is usually the spine. Their backs are simply too long for their little bodies, and, over the years, strain on their spines can lead to back pain and injury.

Some dogs get into trouble not because of their size, shape, or bone structure, but because of what's on the outside—their skin and hair. Skin infections are a problem for breeds such as the bloodhound, Saint Bernard, and Chinese shar-pei, whose skins are very loose and wrinkled. Sagging eyelids sometimes go along with wrinkly coats, so these breeds may also suffer from eye infections.

Eye irritation can afflict Old English sheepdogs, Maltese, and other breeds whose long hair hangs over their faces. And dogs with long, floppy ears, like the cocker spaniel, are more susceptible to ear infections. If you have any of these breeds, be on the lookout for problems. By routinely checking your dog's eyes and ears, or making a trip to the veterinarian as soon as you suspect a skin irritation, you can solve many of your pet's problems before they start.

All the disorders we've just mentioned are examples of what can happen when people select for extreme or outlandish physical characteristics. But selective breeding for a certain behavior or personality can cause problems, too.

Pit bull terriers have been bred for many years as fighting dogs. To be a successful fighter, a pit bull must be aggressive. It must also ignore some of the basic rules of dog behavior. These rules say that, when a dog is faced with an opponent much larger and fiercer than itself, it should give up. When faced with an opponent that shows submissive behavior, it should stop attacking. By following these rules, most dogs are able to stay out of fights and avoid being hurt. But a pit bull bred to fight will keep on fighting, no matter what its opponent does. Because they do not pay attention to the rules of canine behavior, some pit bull terriers have a very hard time getting along with other dogs. And because they insist on winning every contest (whether it is a dogfight or just a disagreement with their owner), they can also be difficult to train.

Not all pit bulls act this way, of course. A pit bull that is not from fighting stock may be as friendly and as easy to train as any other dog. It is the dogs bred for fighting that have given the whole breed a bad name. Unfortunately, many people assume that all pit bulls are vicious, unpredictable killers. As a result, many communities have voted to ban these dogs entirely. In other places, pit bulls must be muzzled whenever they are outdoors.

It seems unfair that the gentle and trainable pit bulls have to suffer because of the breed's reputation. What's even more unfair is that people often blame the dogs for being the way they are. If a pit bull turns out to be an aggressive killer, it is not the dog's fault. Rather, it is the fault of the people who have selected and bred dogs with these qualities. All dogs, from the ferocious pit bull to the tiny, high-strung Chihuahua to the huge Saint Bernard with hip problems are just what humans have made them. In all these cases, a "dog problem" is actually a problem caused by people!

Throughout this book, we have met many different types of dog, from Great Danes to Labrador retrievers to toy poodles. There is one we haven't met, and this dog is probably more popular than all the others combined. It is very adaptable, comes in a wide range of sizes and colors, and can be found all over the world. The dog we're talking about is the mixed breed, or mutt.

Though the pure breeds are great, dogs of mixed ancestry sometimes make even better pets. One reason for this is their adaptability. As we learned, the pure breeds were created to do very specific things—tracking, herding, guarding, and so on. Sometimes, when a dog specializes in doing just one job, it is not very good at other jobs. Retrievers, for example, are wonderful when it comes to fetching things, but they may not be as interested in guarding as a Doberman or a rottweiler would be.

Some dogs are so preoccupied by their special job that they don't pay attention to anything else. To a bloodhound, tracking by smell is all-important. Once this dog begins to follow a scent trail, it is almost impossible to get it to stop.

Mutts are a bit more versatile. A golden retriever-German shepherd mix, for instance, will most likely be friendly, obedient, and playful, and it will probably be a better guard dog than a purebred golden retriever would be.

Another good thing about mixed breeds is that they are less likely to show some of the inherited defects we discussed earlier in this chapter. For instance, a pekapoo (a Pekingese-poodle mix) will probably not have as flat a face as a purebred Pekingese, and so will not suffer as many breathing problems.

Finally, mixed breed dogs are easy to find. To get a good purebred dog, you'll need to look around for a responsible breeder and be prepared to spend several hundred dollars for a puppy. On the other hand, with just one visit to an animal shelter, you'll meet an incredible variety of mixed breed puppies and dogs (along with some purebreds), all looking for good homes. In the United States alone, animal shelters take in millions of dogs each year. Giving one of them a loving home is one of the best things you can do.

Whether you choose a pure breed or a mutt, you're sure to find that a dog is a wonderful companion. And if you know a bit about its history, you'll understand and get along with your pet even better!

APPENDIX

Dog Breeds and Their Original Uses

WORKING DOGS

Akita—Used in Japan for hunting deer, bear, and boar; also as a guard dog.

Alaskan malamute—Pulling sleds. The malamute is noted for its great strength.

Bernese mountain dog—Used by basket weavers in Berne, Switzerland, to haul carts to market.

Boxer—Dogfighting, bull baiting; more recently police work.

Bullmastiff—Originally used by English gamekeepers to catch poachers on large estates. Also known as gamekeeper's night dog.

Doberman pinscher—Guarding and protecting; police and military work.

Great Dane—Boar hunting, guarding.

Great Pyrenees—Guarding sheep in the Pyrenees mountains (between France and Spain).

Komondor—Guarding livestock in the mountains of Hungary.

Kuvasz—Bred in Hungary as a guard dog for royalty.

Mastiff—Fighting and guarding. The huge, powerful mastiff has also been used in wartime.
Newfoundland—Water rescue.
Rottweiler—Driving and protecting cattle; more recently guard and police work.
Saint Bernard—Alpine rescue.
Samoyed—Pulling sleds; herding reindeer.
Siberian husky—Pulling sleds.

HERDING DOGS

Border collie—Herding sheep.
Bouvier des Flandres—Herding cattle.
Briard—Guarding and herding livestock.
Collie—Herding.
German shepherd—Herding; more recently police work and guide-dog work.
Old English sheepdog—Herding, guarding, and driving livestock to market.
Puli—Herding.
Shetland sheepdog—Herding sheep.
Welsh corgi—Driving cattle.

HOUNDS

Afghan hound—Hunting leopards and gazelles.
Basenji—Hunting. The name of this barkless African hunting dog means "savage."
Basset hound—Slow trailing of rabbits and other prey hunted on foot.
Beagle—Hunting rabbits and hares.
Bloodhound—Originally used for hunting stags. More recently used to track missing persons.
Borzoi—Hunting wolves and other animals on the steppes of Russia.
Dachshund—Hunting badgers.
Foxhound (American and English)—Used in packs to hunt foxes.

Greyhound—Hunting; racing.
Irish wolfhound—Hunting wolves in Ireland.
Norwegian elkhound—A Nordic dog, used to hunt elk and other large game.
Rhodesian ridgeback—Used to hunt large game in Africa. Sometimes known as the African lion dog.
Saluki—Hunting gazelles and antelope.
Scottish deerhound—Hunting deer.
Whippet—Developed specifically for racing.

SPORTING DOGS

Standard pointer—Stalking birds and indicating their location by freezing in place with nose pointed toward the hidden game ("pointing").
German pointer (short-haired and wire-haired)—Stalking and pointing birds.
Chesapeake Bay retriever—Retrieving fallen game from the water.
Golden retriever—Retrieving game in water and on land. Also used as a guide dog.
Labrador retriever—Retrieving game in water and on land. Also used as a guide dog.
English setter—Locating game and indicating its location by dropping to the ground ("setting").
Irish setter—Locating and setting game.
Gordon setter—Locating and setting game.
Cocker spaniel (American and English)—Tracking birds and flushing them out of the underbrush. The cocker spaniel gets its name from the bird it specializes in hunting, the woodcock.
Springer spaniel (English and Welsh)—Tracking and flushing birds.
Water spaniel (American and Irish)—Retrieving game from the water.
Vizsla—Stalking, pointing, and retrieving game.
Weimaraner—Stalking, pointing, and retrieving game. The Weimaraner and the Vizsla are considered "multipurpose" hunting dogs because they can do a variety of jobs for the hunter.

TERRIERS

Airedale—Hunting medium-sized animals such as otters, foxes, and badgers.
American Staffordshire terrier/Staffordshire bull terrier—Fighting.
Bedlington terrier—Hunting small animals.
Border terrier—Hunting. Named for its place of origin: the border counties between England and Scotland.
Bull terrier—Bull baiting, dogfighting.
Cairn terrier—Hunting small animals in Scotland's rocky cairns.
Dandie Dinmont terrier—Hunting small animals.
Fox terrier—Hunting foxes.
Irish terrier—Hunting small animals.
Kerry blue terrier—Hunting, retrieving, and herding. The Kerry blue terrier is named for its place of origin, County Kerry in Ireland.
Lakeland terrier—Hunting foxes and other animals. Originated in England's Lake District.
Manchester terrier—Catching rats.
Norfolk terrier—Hunting small animals, such as rats and rabbits.
Scottish terrier—Hunting foxes, ferrets, and other medium-sized animals.
Sealyham terrier—Hunting badgers, otters, and foxes.
Skye terrier—Hunting small animals.
West Highland white terrier—Hunting small animals.
Soft-coated Wheaten terrier—Hunting and guarding.

TOY DOGS

Affenpinscher—Sometimes called the "monkey terrier." Originally used to catch rats; now kept as pets.
Brussels griffon—Catching rats; now kept as pets.
Chihuahua—Originally used by Mexico's Aztec Indians as food and for religious purposes; now kept as pets.
English toy spaniel—Pets.
Italian greyhound—Pets.

Japanese spaniel—Pets.
Maltese—Pets.
Toy Manchester terrier—Pets.
Miniature pinscher—Pets.
Papillon—Pets.
Pekingese—Pets. Pekingese dogs were the favorite pets of the Chinese emperors.
Pomeranian—Pets.
Toy poodle—Pets.
Pug—Pets.
Shih Tzu—Pets.
Silky terrier—Pets.
Yorkshire terrier—Pets.

NONSPORTING DOGS (a miscellaneous category)

Bichon frise—Pets.
Boston terrier—Pets.
Bulldog—Bull baiting.
Chow chow—Guarding and hunting. This Chinese breed is known for it's blue-black tongue.
Dalmatian—Traditionally used as coach dogs and, later, as firehouse dogs.
French bulldog—Pets.
Keeshond—Originally kept as pets by Dutch barge captains.
Lhasa apso—Pets.
Poodle—Retrieving game from the water.
Schipperke—A Belgian breed used as watchdogs on boats. The breed's name comes from the Flemish word for "skipper."
Tibetan terrier—Pets. Tibetan terriers were highly prized by ancient Tibetan lamas.

INDEX

Active submission, 35–36
Afghan hound, 14, 52, 74, 75
Airedale, 91, 93
Alaskan malamute, 11–12, 53, 55
All-Alaska Sweepstakes, 55
Alpha wolves, 6, 34, 35
American Kennel Club, 20, 53, 55, 86, 92
American Staffordshire terrier, 94
Australian shepherd, 67

Barking, 10, 33, 45–46
Basenji, 10
Basset hound, 10, 23, 78–79
Beagle, 22, 23, 78
Bichon frise, 99
Bird dogs, 81–89
Black-and-tan terrier, 60
Bloodhounds, 14, 22, 23, 39, 77, 108, 110
Body language, 6, 34–37
Border collie, 67, 68
Borzoi, 22, 74–75
Boston terrier, 86
Briard, 66
Brittany spaniel, 84
Bull and terrier, 94
Bull baiting, 20, 94
Bulldog, 20, 52, 86, 94
Bullmastiff, 59–60
Bull terrier, 20, 94

Cairn terrier, 91, 92–93
Cardigan Welsh corgi, 67
Carnivores, 29

Cattle dogs, 59
Chase response, 39–40, 72
Chesapeake Bay retriever, 86
Chewing, 44, 46
Chihuahua, 99, 106
Clumber spaniel, 84
Cocker spaniel, 10, 25, 82, 84, 88, 108
Collie, 15, 67, 68
Communication, 32–33
  by body language, 6, 34–37
  by smell, 37–38
  by sound, 33–34
Companion breeds, 97–102
Continental clip, 87–88
Cooling system, 106
Coonhound, 23
Corgi, 67, 108
Crate, 46
Curly-coated retriever, 86

Dachshund, 78–79, 108
Deerhound, 74, 76
Dobermann, Ludwig, 60
Doberman pinscher, 60
Dogfighting, 20, 94
Dog racing, 75
Domestication, 3–7

Ears, 10, 22, 75, 108
Eating, 40–41
English setter, 82
English toy spaniel, 106
Eye dogs, 68
Eyes, 75, 107–8

117

Face, 106–7
Face licking, 36
Fighting, 56–57
Foxhound, 23, 77–78
Fox terrier, 19, 91

Gaze hounds, 14, 73
German shepherd, 10, 70–72
Golden retriever, 86, 110
Gordon setter, 82
Great Dane, 53, 60, 74, 108
Great Pyrenees, 58–59, 62, 65
Greyhound, 14, 40, 74, 75, 76, 78, 84, 91, 97
Growling, 33–34
Guard dogs, 14, 17–18, 59–64
Gun dogs, 81–82, 84–86

Hackles, raised, 34
Hair, 108
Ha pa dogs, 19
Herding dogs, 14–15, 40, 65–72, 113
Hip dysplasia, 108
Hounds, 14, 73–80, 113–14
House pets, 18–19
Howling, 33, 43–44, 46, 80
Hunting, 7, 38–40
Hunting dogs, 12–14, 19–20, 22–24, 73–80
Huskies, 10, 11–12, 31, 53, 55, 56, 105

Irish setter, 82, 88
Irish terrier, 93
Irish water spaniel, 86
Irish wolfhound, 22, 65, 74, 76
Italian greyhound, 97

Kennel crate, 46
Kerry blue terrier, 93
Komondor, 58–59, 65

Labrador retriever, 62, 85, 86
Lhasa apso, 19, 98

Lion clip, 87–88
Little Red Riding Hood, 29

Malamute, 11–12, 53, 55, 56
Malcolm, E. D., 93
Maltese, 18, 97, 98–99, 108
Manchester terrier, 19–20, 92, 93
Marking of territory, 37–38, 45
Mastiff, 14, 17–18, 57–58
Mech, David, 38, 40
Miniature breeds, 18–19, 98–102
Mixed breeds, 110–11
Mutt, 110–11

Newfoundland, 62
Nonsporting dogs, 116
Norfolk terrier, 92
Nose, 106

Obedience training, 63, 100
Old English sheepdog, 66, 68–70, 108
Old English terrier, 94

Panting, 75
Pariah dogs, 11
Passive submission, 34–35
Pekapoo, 110
Pekingese, 19, 97, 98, 105, 106
Pembroke Welsh corgi, 67
Pit bull terrier, 20, 94, 109
Pointer, 25, 84
Polar dogs, 11–12, 53–57
Poodle, 86–88, 97, 100–101, 106
Prey, 39–40
Problems, 105–11
Pug, 106

Racing, 55, 75
Rat catcher, 20, 93
Red Riding Hood, 29
Rescue dogs, 60–62
Retriever, 25, 84–86, 110
Rottweiler, 59
Russian wolfhound, 22, 74–75

Index

Saint Bernard, 60–62, 108
Saint John's dogs, 85
Salukis, 40, 73, 74
Samoyed, 11–12, 53, 55, 56
Scavengers, 5, 6, 11
Scent hounds, 14, 22–24, 77–80
Scent marking, 37–38, 45
Scottish deerhound, 74, 76
Scottish terrier, 91, 92
Sealyham terrier, 93
Selective breeding, 8–10, 15, 105–11
Setters, 22, 25, 82
Setting spaniel, 82
Shar-pei, 108
Sheepdogs, 15, 58–59, 65–79
Shetland sheepdog, 15, 67, 68
Shih Tzu, 19
Siberian husky, 11–12, 53, 55, 105
Sight hounds, 14, 22, 73–76
Skin, 108
Skye terrier, 91, 92
Sled dogs, 11–12, 53–57
   racing, 55
Sleeve dogs, 19, 97
Smell, 12–14, 39
   communicating by, 37–38
Soiling, 45–46
Sound, communicating by, 33–34
Spaniel, 22, 25, 82–84, 106
Spine, 108
Sporting dogs, 22–25, 81–89, 114
Springer spaniel, 25, 82, 84
Staffordshire bull terrier, 92, 94
Stalking, 39
Submission, 34–36

Tail, 9
   wagging, 35–36

Talbot hound, 78
Teacup poodle, 106
Teeth, 107
Terrier, 19–20, 25, 60, 64, 90–96, 98, 100–101, 115
Three Little Pigs, 29
Tibetan terrier, 98
Toy dogs, 18–19, 98–102, 106, 115–16
Toy poodle, 97, 100–101, 106
Toy spaniel, 106
Training, 45–46, 63, 100

Vizsla, 84

Watchdogs, 7, 80, 96, 102
Water retrievers, 86–88
Weimaraner, 84
Welsh corgi, 67, 108
Welsh terrier, 93
Werewolf, 29–30
Whippet, 75
White cairn terrier, 93
White terrier, 93
Wire kennel crate, 46
Wolf dogs, 12
Wolfhound, 22, 65, 74–76
Wolves, 29–32
   communication, 32–38
   eating, 40–41
   and humans, 5–7
   hunting, 38–40
   selective breeding, 8–10
Working dogs, 53–64, 112–13

Yorkshire terrier, 100–101

PICTURE CREDITS: pages 12, 17, 18, 21, 23, New York Public Library Picture Collection; page 13, The Metropolitan Museum of Art, gift of John D. Rockefeller, Jr., 1937 (37.80.1); page 15, *Illustrated London News*/New York Public Library Picture Collection; pages 24, 43, 44, 54, 58, 61, 66, 71 (top), 78, 79, 83, 85, 87, 92, 98, 107 (left), ASPCA; page 30, New York Zoological Society; page 71 (bottom), U.S. Customs; pages 69, 95, 101, 107 (right), Mary Bloom.